501 FACTS FACTORY

AMAZING BUILDINGS OF THE WORLD

Sreelata Menon is an author, freelance writer and history buff, who shuttles between Gurugram and Bengaluru. With many children's books to her credit, she especially enjoys introducing children to the rich cultural and historical heritage of our past. She believes that only through knowledge of their inherited legacy can children be inspired to make a viable future for themselves – like any building that stands tall, the foundation needs to be strong, firm and informed.

501 FACTS FACTORY

AMAZING BUILDINGS OF THE WORLD

Sreelata Menon

hachette INDIA

First published in 2019 by Hachette India
(Registered name: Hachette Book Publishing India Pvt. Ltd)
An Hachette UK company
www.hachetteindia.com

SRD

ISBN 978-93-88322-27-0

Hachette Book Publishing India Pvt. Ltd
4th & 5th Floors, Corporate Centre
Plot No. 94, Sector 44, Gurugram - 122003, India

Typeset by Manmohan Kumar, Delhi

Printed and bound in India
by Manipal Technologies Limited

MIX
Paper from responsible sources
FSC™ C043100

CONTENTS

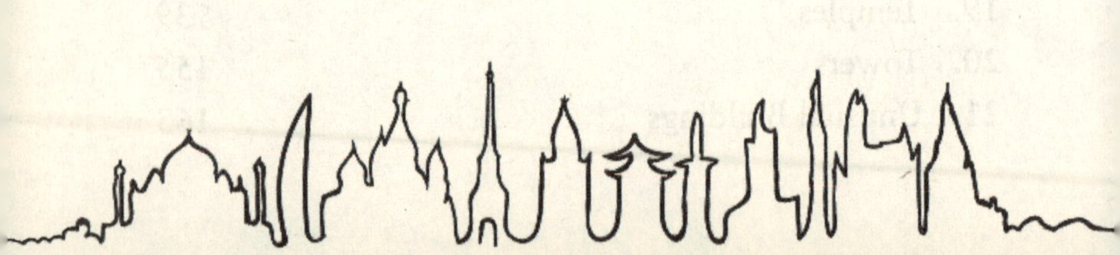

1

ARCHITECTURE

Over the ages many styles of architecture have developed across the world. Every civilization and country worked out its own styles, and categories within those, which continued to be embellished and modified.

1 **The word 'architect' comes from the Greek word '*archi+tekton*' meaning chief carpenter.**

2 **'Vastu Shastra' or the 'science of architecture' dates back to the Vedic period in (c. 2000 to 600 BCE) India.** Its designs combine building with Nature, and match the functions of parts of a structure with beliefs about patterns, symmetry, space arrangement and directions.

3 **As early as the 11th century, Chinese architect Li Jie compiled the *Yingzao Fashi*, a technical manual on Chinese architecture.** This book became a success during the Song Dynasty rule, and Li Jie was made the Director of Palace Buildings by Emperor Huizong.

4 **One of the world's first acknowledged architects was Imhotep in Egypt.** He was also a doctor! He designed the first square-based step pyramid tomb at Saqqara in the 3rd century for the Egyptian Pharaoh Djoser, and had his name inscribed next to the pharaoh's! He also wrote an architectural encyclopedia that guided Egyptian builders for thousands of years after his death.

5 **Architecture was once worthy of an Olympic medal!** Baron Pierre de Coubertin founded the International Olympic Committee in 1894 and, along with athletics, swimming and team sports, medals were given to sports-related entries in arts and architecture too. Dutch architect Jan Wils won the 1928 Olympic gold for architecture, for designing the very stadium that hosted the 1928 Games. The arts awards were discontinued after the 1948 London Games.

6 **The ancient Greeks perfected the architecture of columns in their temples, using posts and lintels.** Dedicated to the Goddess Athena, the famous Parthenon, built in 432 BCE, has rows and rows of white pillars or columns (70 of them!) holding up the roof. These columns were in three styles – Doric, Ionic and Corinthian. The Doric style is rather sturdy and its top is plain. The Ionic style is more elegant and decorated on top with a scroll-like design (a volute). In the Corinthian style, the top is very elaborate and decorated with acanthus (a poppy-like flower) leaves.

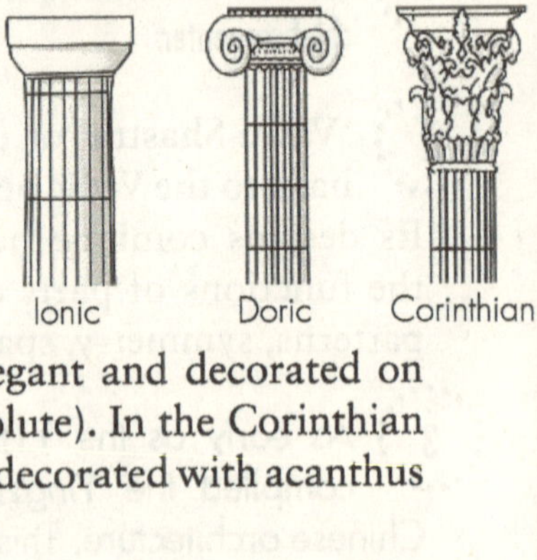

7 **Ancient Rome built upon the ideas of the Greeks, developed Roman concrete and gave us vaults, domes and arches.** Imagine a crowd of 80,000 roaring spectators on their feet, watching a gladiator fight as long ago as 72 CE in the Colosseum, an oval sporting area in ancient Rome (now in Italy). With its 80 arched entrances, it was once the world's largest amphitheatre built by Emperor Vespasian. It was 620 ft long, 183 ft wide and about 12 storeys high.

8 Here are a few of the main styles of architecture:

– **Gothic** architecture specializes in stained glass and rose windows, vaults, buttresses (a structure extending out to support the wall), clustered columns, wheel windows, spires and carved semicircular or triangular decorative wall surface designs over the door. All these can be seen in the Cathedral of Notre-Dame, Paris, France.

– **Baroque** architecture typically features clusters of sculpted angels and gilded figures on the ceiling with painted figures on the walls. With twisting columns, it includes light coming from bronze and gilded cupolas for dramatic effects as at the Schonbrunn Palace, Austria.

– **Hindu** architecture features carved gopurams or conical/pyramidal/mountain-shaped domes atop temples. They have exquisitely decorated sculptures and carvings related to the presiding deity, as in the temples in Kanchipuram, Tamil Nadu, India.

– **Islamic** architecture includes Persian, Moorish and Mughal styles with pointed arches, onion-shaped domes, courtyards and minarets, as at the Char Minar in Hyderabad, India.

– **Byzantine** architecture uses domes, semi-domes, and windowed domes that look like a crown with jewels of light. The last type developed during the 6th century reign of Emperor Justinian I, as at the Hagia Sophia in Istanbul, Turkey, which was a church for the first 1,000 years.

– **Renaissance** architecture indulges in large buildings with huge classical motifs, arches, large domes, statues, Roman-type columns and arcades, as in St. Peter's Basilica in Rome, Italy.

– The **Art Noveau** style features ornamental flower stalks and buds, vine tendrils, insect wings – all from Nature – as in architect Gaudi's Casa Battlo in Barcelona, Spain.

– The **Neoclassical** style revels in the dramatic use of columns, blank walls and simple geometric forms, but grand in scale, as in the US Capitol Building in Washington, D.C.

– The **Art Deco** style features rectangular and curved lines, strong geometric shapes and vibrant colours as in the Chrysler Building, New York, USA.

Door of Dolmabahce Palace

– The **Rococo** style is all about elaborate ornamentation, pastel colours and serpent-like lines as in the Dolmabahce Palace in Istanbul, Turkey.

– The **Romanesque** style include stylized floral and tree/leaf stone decorations, twisted rope designs around doors and rounded arches as in the churches of Cologne, Germany.

– The **Southeast Asian** style specializes in curved roofs, wooden structures and rich artistic images on the roof, as in the Forbidden City in Beijing, China.

– The **Modernistic** style has low functional buildings, as at the Indian Institute of Management, Ahmedabad, India.

9 **There are eco-friendly architectural materials being developed.** For instance, mycelium is a futuristic building material that has the root structure of fungi and mushrooms! It can be grown around natural materials, like straw, and then air-dried to create lightweight and strong bricks.

10 **There are many new techniques under research as well.** One such is Grasscrete, which is a method of laying concrete flooring, walkways, sidewalks and driveways that allow grass or other flora to grow. It reduces concrete usage and helps water drainage.

2

CASTLES

The medieval period in Europe witnessed endless conflicts, and rulers and noblemen built themselves fortified palaces called castles. Coming from the Latin word '*castellum*', meaning 'fortified place', castles were centres of great power and security. Housing large swathes of the local people, many feudal lords or noblemen owned more than one castle and a monarch many.

11 **The first castles were built by the Normans (1066–1215), who invaded England, and were called 'motte and bailey castles'.** Early castles used mostly earth and timber. Later, through the centuries, they were so heavily fortified that they actually became fortresses.

12 **William the Conqueror built nine motte and bailey castles in England.** The most important part of the castle was a wooden or stone 'keep' tower in the centre. This is where the Lord lived. Built on an enormous man-made raised earth mound called a motte, it had an enclosed ward, courtyard or 'bailey' around it, surrounded by a protective ditch or 'moat' filled with water. The moat had a 'drawbridge' that could be pulled up to deny access to the castle. It also had a 'palisade' or fence. The walls were high and heavy, and the doors were massive, with iron studs.

13 **Early castles had distinctive features.** A spiked wooden or metal barrier, called 'portcullis', helped protect the doors of the motte and bailey castle from fire and battering. It had a 'battlement', a protective tooth-shaped parapet with a walk behind it for the soldiers to stand on. The defenders could fire through gaps. The raised sections between, sheltered the defenders during an enemy attack.

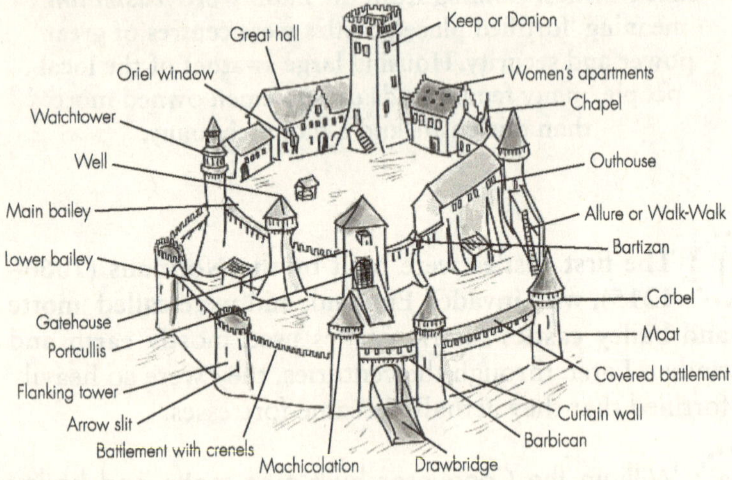

Parts of a Medieval Castle

14 **Motte and bailey castles had lookout towers called 'turrets' and stone boxes that projected from the walls.** They had holes on the floors called 'machicolations' for dropping stones, boiling oil or tar on attackers. Tall, thick 'curtain walls' surrounded the castle buildings like a strong shield. Some castles had flanking towers as well. Nearly all later castles were improved versions of this model, which included concentric castles that had walls within walls.

Portcullis

15 **Beaumaris Castle in North Wales has the most number of portcullises, six of them.** There are three portcullises for each of its two gatehouses. These spiked wooden or metal barriers could be lowered by chains from a chamber above the gateway.

16 **Windsor Castle in the English county of Berkshire is the oldest and largest inhabited castle in the world.** It was built as a motte-and-bailey by William the Conqueror in 1060. With three wards surrounding a central mound that was gradually replaced with stone fortifications and heavy stone walls 13 ft thick, Windsor Castle is an official residence of the Queen of England. It has been home to about 30 sovereigns over 900 years. It has about 1,000 sumptuously decorated rooms spread over 13 acres of land. Its many dungeons have had many famous prisoners too.

17 **Windsor Castle is also home to part of the largest art collection in the world owned by the British royal family.** The royal library contains more than 200,000 items, including the book collections of multiple monarchs.

Windsor Castle (1670s)

18 **Queen Mary's Doll's House in Windsor Castle is the world's largest and most elaborate miniature home within a home.** It has running water, electricity, flush toilets, elevators, a fully-stocked 1200-piece wine cellar with real wine and beer, and a miniature library filled with original stories handwritten by authors like Rudyard Kipling and Sir Arthur Conan Doyle. Designed and gifted to Queen Mary in 1920 by Edwin Lutyens, it had more than 1,500 craftsmen and artists work on it.

19 **The Pena National Palace in Lisbon, Spain, built by King Ferdinand II in 1842, is a colourful mix of many architectural styles.** A medley of yellow, purple and pink pastel colours gives it a fairy-tale look. Atop the Sintra Mountains and spread over 20 hectares of park and forest, its walls carry symbolic carvings, Biblical stories and religious figures along with lavishly painted Portuguese tiles. It has two gateways and a drawbridge as well as a clock tower. Inside is a mixture of ornate stuccos (plaster), multi-patterned columns and Moorish arched ceilings. It is still used for state occasions.

20 **Nottingham Castle is a motte and bailey castle built in 1068, by William the Conqueror, on top of 'castle rock' overlooking the city of Nottingham, UK.** Robin Hood, the popular local hero supposedly held captive in Nottingham Castle by the Sheriff of Nottingham, is said to have escaped to the nearby Sherwood Forest through the caves and tunnels below, many of which are still there. The mansion that stands in place of the medieval castle now is a museum and art gallery.

Prague Castle

21 **Prague Castle in Czechoslovakia, built in the 9th century, is actually a castle complex with stone palaces, churches and houses, spread over 750,000 sq. ft.** It has a singing fountain in the middle of the Royal Garden next to the beautiful Royal Gazebo. The present seat of the government and one-time power base of the Bohemian kings and Holy Roman emperors, the castle complex today houses the crown jewels of the Bohemian royals in its secret chambers.

22 **Tintagel Castle, King Arthur's supposed home in Cornwall, England, was built in 1150 near the sea by Reginald, the Earl of Cornwall.** Though there is no sign of the famed Round Table, there is a natural depression in the rocks near the castle, which is called Arthur's Footprint. Nearby is Merlin's Cave where Merlin supposedly carried the baby Arthur at high tide.

23 **The Tower of London, UK, an irregularly shaped concentric castle built in 1066 by William the Conqueror, is now a UNESCO heritage site.** Though built as a royal residence, it was used as a prison and was

a symbol of oppression. The oldest part of the fortress is the White Tower, and the 90 ft high keep was the tallest in London for a long time. Over 23,500 pieces of the Crown Jewels are also housed within. It has 21 towers in all and the tower walls, about 110 to120 ft long on any side, are about 11 to 15 ft thick.

Tower of London (15th century)

24 **Most castles did not have toilets! One had to aim at small holes called 'garderobes', which then carried the muck down to the moats.**

25 **'Dracula's Castle' in author Bram Stoker's vampire story was a take-off on the 13th century Bran Castle in Transylvania in present-day Romania.** Situated at Bran on the border between Transylvania and Wallachia near the city of Brasov, Bran Castle is a national monument and landmark. Perched on a cliff at a height of 2,500 ft, and surrounded by valleys and hills, the castle has narrow stairways that lead through a total of only 60 rooms all made of timber.

Bran Castle

26 **Was Bran Castle really Dracula's castle? Who knows!** But a 'Vlad Dracula' who happened to like the taste of blood was probably imprisoned in Bran Castle for some time, before being transferred to the prison near Budapest in present-day Hungary. He was probably the inspiration for author Bram Stoker's Dracula.

27 **Walt Disney's Sleeping Beauty's Castle was inspired by the Castle Neuschwanstein, built in 1892 by Ludwig II of Bavaria.** The 'Fairy Tale King' as he was known, wanted a fairy-tale castle complete with beautiful views of the Bavarian Alps. Over 400,000 bricks and about 5,000 tonnes of marble were used and numerous paintings inspired by characters from operas decorate the walls. Neuschwanstein itself is taken from the 'Swan Knight', a character in one of the German composer Wagner's operas. Ludwig slept only 11 nights in the castle and died before it was completed.

Castle Neuschwanstein

28 **Gun powder, invented in 1320, brought about a decline in castle building.** Wood and stone castle fortifications were no match for booming cannons and heavy artillery fire. The Byzantine–Christian Empire came to an end in 1453, mainly with the fall of the heavily fortified city of Constantinople to the Muslim Ottoman Emperor Mehmet II who used huge cannons to demolish the city walls.

29 **The trebuchet was a siege weapon that was a seesaw with a huge weight at one end and a sling with a stone at the other, which when released could damage castle walls.**

30 **The best-preserved moated castle in Europe, Egeskov Castle, Denmark, has a moat that is an entire lake.** The castle, supported by oak pilings, sits atop the 16 ft

deep lake. It took a whole forest of oak trees to build the foundation, hence the name Egeskov meaning 'oak forest'. Access was only by drawbridge. It has 66 rooms, 171 doors, more than 2,000 windowpanes, a farm, a car museum, and a finely detailed doll's house.

Egeskov Castle

31 **First it was a Roman lighthouse, then it was a church and finally the strategically placed Dover Castle, rebuilt in 1066 by William the Conqueror, became one of the largest castles in England.** Guarding the Straits of Dover, the crossing point from Calais in France, it has been proudly perched on top of the White Cliffs overlooking the busy port of Dover for over 2,000 years. With its massive gates, portcullis, drawbridge and baileys intact, this stone castle's 80 ft tall and almost 100 ft square 'Great Tower' is the largest and most expensive keep ever built in England. Behind its battlements there is an underground lair with a vast network of tunnels used as air shelters and a defensive nerve centre during the World Wars.

32 **Japan's Marugame Castle is a rock castle built between 1558 and 1600.** Overlooking the Seto Inland Sea, it is one of the country's famous 12 castles and its walls are the highest in the world. As high as a 20-storey building, its walls are curvy, with carvings. Famous for its cherry blossoms, the castle has nearly 1,000 cherry trees planted around the walls and castle keep. It still has its original wooden *tenshu* (keep) built before 1860. The castle is located now in Kameyama Park, with a museum in the *tenshu*.

3

CHURCHES

The church building or church house is often designed in the shape of a Christian cross in traditional Christian architecture. The longest part of a cross is represented by the aisle of the structure and the altar area is placed at the junction of the cross.

33 **Designed by architect Sir Christopher Wren, the St. Paul's Cathedral in London, UK, took 35 years to build.** Begun in 1675 and completed by Wren's son in 1710, it is a combination of Neoclassical, Gothic and Baroque styles. Its magnificent cross, 365 ft above ground, stands atop the second largest dome in the world – St Peter's Basilica's in Rome being the largest. It was the tallest building in London from 1710 to 1967. A circular walkway at the base of the dome – the 'whispering gallery' – allows the softest of whispers to be heard at the opposite wall of the cathedral, 112 ft away.

34 **St. Paul's Cathedral is the fourth functioning church to stand on its site.** First built in 604 CE, it was destroyed by fire, rebuilt, destroyed by the Vikings, and built once more before again being burnt to a crisp in the Great Fire of London in 1666, after which Sir Wren recreated it using iron and stone. This grand church has over 200 monuments and memorials of many great British men in its crypt. Sir

St. Paul's Cathedral

Wren himself is buried here. The Duke of Wellington (who defeated Napoleon at Waterloo and was twice prime minister of England) on horseback is the largest statue in the cathedral. As many as 530 steps take you to the Golden Gallery, an observation platform atop the dome. With Victorian mosaics and many sculptures, this cathedral has history written all over its walls. It was also here that Prince Charles married Princess Diana in 1981.

35 **'Our Lady of the Snows' is a Catholic chapel carved out of ice in Argentine Antarctica. It is one among eight churches in the Antarctica.**

36 **An ancient chapel that will shock and dismay is the Capela dos Ossos in Evora, Portugal.** In a small chapel at the entrance of the Church of St. Francis, the walls and eight pillars inside are covered with human skulls and bones cemented together. The ceiling of white painted brick has death motifs painted on it. There are also 5,000 skeletons that appear to have been collected from nearby cemeteries. The message? That life is just a short stay in this world.

37 **St. Peter's Basilica, the largest and grandest Catholic Church in the world, is in the Vatican in Rome, Italy, with the Pope as its head.** Built of travertine stone and spread over 240,000 sq. ft, the basilica (a church granted special rights) is

St. Peter's Basilica

448.1 ft high, 730 ft long and 500 ft wide. It was built over the tomb of St. Peter, one of the twelve Apostles of Jesus Christ. It has been designed in the shape of a Greek cross (all sides equal) with a dome at the point where it crosses over the shrine of St. Peter the Apostle.

38 **The golden dome of the St. Peter's Basilica is the largest in the world.** Designed by the famous painter and sculptor Michelangelo, it is 136.1 ft in diameter and 434.7 ft high. As many as 491 steps lead up to its top. All the paintings on the walls are actually mosaics.

39 **Just below the St. Peter's Basilica dome is the magnificent 96 ft – 10 storeys high – black bronze 'Baldacchino' or four-poster canopy over the altar.** Made of 100,000 pounds of bronze, it was taken from the Pantheon in Rome in 1653.

40 **Built in 1506, St Peter's Basilica has more than 100 eminent people buried in its crypts.** It has many gigantic statues too, 150 of them of saints, standing 5 m tall in niches of pillars in the colonnade outside. Inside, 'The Pieta', the most famous sculpture of Jesus on the lap of his mother Mary, is kept in bulletproof glass.

41 **There are some words written around the dome of St Peter's Basilica.** Since c. 30 CE there have been 266 Popes in all so far, with Pope Francis I being the current one.

Catholics believe that Popes are symbolic descendants of St. Peter, the first Pope appointed by Jesus Christ himself as his representative on earth. *'Thou art Peter and upon this rock I will build my church,'* says Christ in the Bible. *'I will give to thee the keys of the kingdom of heaven.'* And these words are written around the dome.

42 **Built by Emperor Constantine I himself over St Paul the Apostle's grave is the cathedral of St. Paul's Outside the Walls in Rome, Italy.** In this 4th century church there are a number of papal friezes (stone frames with portraits of Popes who have passed on). There are today only six empty spaces left. It is believed that the sixth Pope from now will be the last Pope, before the world comes to an end!

43 **With a quirky name like 'Reading Between the Lines', a church in Borgloon, Belgium, is extraordinary.** It is made up of 100 layers of stacked steel on a concrete platform. With each layer separated from the other by more than 2,000 squat steel columns, the walls seem semi-transparent, but from a lower or higher angle they appear solid and the building weighs 30 tonnes. Designed by Gijs Van Vaerenbergh in 2011 as a piece of modern art, it welcomes all worshippers.

44 **Nearly 1,800 fir poles, 600 chestnut branches and 19,685 ft of hazel branches joined together with wood, nails and string form the Cattedrale Vegetale or Tree Cathedral in Bergamo, Italy.** As many as 42 beech trees have been planted to grow over this structure and eventually form 42 columns to create a basilica of five aisles after the poles and branches decay. Spread over 650 sq. m, it is more than 90 feet long, 80 feet wide, and ranges in height from about 16 to 70 ft. An amazing piece of natural architecture, it was created by Italian architect Giuliano Mauri in 2010.

45 **A rather unusual church is the Chene Chapelle or Chapel Oak in northern France.** It is inside an enormous oak tree, as old as the Kingdom of France, they say. However, it is at least 800 years old and a spiral staircase around it takes you to two tiny separate chapels within it. The hollow of the tree was struck by lightning in the 17th century and was converted into a church by the local priest.

Chene Chapelle

46 **The world's first Inflatable Church was erected in Sandown, England. Built in 2003, it is 47 ft high, 47ft long and 25ft wide, and can hold 60 worshippers. Like all churches, it has an altar, a pulpit, an organ, and stained-glass windows too. Created by Michael Gill, everything in it is inflatable, including the candles!**

Lalibela churches

47 **Hewn into the rocky hills of Lalibela in Ethiopia are some extraordinary underground churches.** Carved out of single rocks in the 13th century, there are 13 of them, each 33 ft tall and 108 ft long, connected by passages 36 ft deep. The Lalibela Rock Churches, a UNESCO Heritage site, are huge, with prayer halls, vaults, pillars, doors and windows, and the complex appears to represent Jerusalem. It must have taken about 24 years to carve them out of volcanic rock after, they say, an angel told the King Lalibela to erect them. They were discovered by a Portuguese priest in 1520.

48 **A fascinating mix of the old and the modern is the Temppeliaukio Church or Church of the Rock in Helsinki, Finland.** Built in 1968 in a massive piece of granite, this cave-like place of worship was designed by architect brothers Timo and Tuomo Suomalainen. With walls blasted from inside and a stunning copper dome roof, it has 180 vertical glass window panes that let natural light in and make it seem like the dome floats.

49 **After the Pyramid of Giza, which was the tallest building for 3,800 years, Lincoln's Cathedral in England was the world's tallest building for the next 238 years from 1311 to 1548.** In that year its spire collapsed and was never rebuilt. Built over 54,000 sq. ft by William the Conqueror, it has rose windows, decorative motifs and, most specially, a stone figure of an imp. Let loose

by the Devil to create havoc in the church, the story goes, the imps or little devils were smashing windows and ruining lights. An angel asked them to stop, but one imp wouldn't listen and was turned to stone high up among its walls on a pillar. This 12-inch figure, known as the Lincoln Imp, is the city's symbol. The Lincoln City football club's nickname is the Imps too.

Lincoln Imp

50 **Several hundreds of feet underground, carved out of rock salt, are chapels in the salt mines of Wieliczka in Poland.** In existence since the 13th century, new ones are created, with the old ones being demolished once the salt is excavated. Five main chapels exist currently, one of which is dedicated to Pope John Paul II, who has often visited them. It boasts of a salt sculpture of the Pope.

51 **The largest Gothic-style church in the world is the Seville Cathedral in Spain.** It is also the third largest cathedral in the world. Covered in gold, 45 scenes from the life of Christ can be found carved in wood on the world's richest and largest altar here. Spread over some 124,000 sq. ft, this Roman Catholic cathedral has 80 chapels and 15 doors. Among its rich paintings and fabulous architectural artifacts, there is also a crocodile model known as El Lagarto, a wooden crocodile covered with the skin of a real one gifted by the Sultan of Egypt to the daughter of King Alfonso X. The tomb of explorer Christopher Columbus also lies here.

52 **The oldest church in India is the Palayur Church in Cranganore or Kodungalloor as it is known now.** It was

built by St. Thomas, one of the twelve apostles of Jesus Christ, after he landed in Kerala in 52 CE. Though the outside walls were rebuilt in the 17th century, the altar, consecrated by St Thomas, remains.

53 **The Etchmiadzin Cathedral is 1,717 years old and still going strong.** The world's first cathedral, built by the state between 310 and 303 CE, is in Armenia, the world's first Christian country. It is now the headquarters of the Armenian Apostolic Church.

54 **Designed by architect Oscar Niemeyer and opened in 1970, the Cathedral of Brasília in Brasilia, Brazil, is a fascinating modern building.** Sixteen curved concrete columns first meet inwards before flaring outwards at the top, giving the impression of a huge white crown with pointed ends. Each of those columns weighs 90 tonnes and is 131 ft tall. Four bronze sculptures, each 9.8 ft, representing the Four Evangelists, Matthew, Mark, Luke, and John, guard the entrance.

55 **Designed to resemble Iceland's natural landscape of volcanoes, ice caps and basalt columns is the Church of Hallgrimskirkja in Reykjavik.** It was completed in 1974 after 38 years. It stands 244 ft tall on a hill in the centre of the city, an amazing upside-down V, made up of thin white beams. Built of poured cement, it is named after Iceland's famous 17th century poet and clergyman Hallgrimur Petursson.

Church of Hallgrimskirkja

4

CLOCK TOWERS

Chances are that you will bump into a clock tower or two in every city. Some stand squarely in the middle of the city at road junctions as if directing traffic, others on building facades or in public gardens. They were at first simple striking clocks to call people to work or prayer.

56 **The Tower of the Winds in Athens, Greece, dated to around 50 BCE, is the earliest clock the world has known.** It had eight sundials and a water clock, which was driven by water flowing from the Acropolis.

Tower of the Winds (18th century model)

57 **Heard about the clock in the nursery rhyme?** 'Hickory, dickory, dock, the mouse ran up the clock…' Guess which clock it went up and down? Andrew Lang, author of the 1897 *The Nursery Rhyme Book*, based it on the astronomical clock at Exeter Cathedral in England. It displays the hour of the day, the day of the lunar month and the phase of the moon. A small bell behind the dial chimes every quarter of an hour. The clock has a small hole in the door below the face for cats to hunt mice since old cathedrals usually have mice.

Prague Orloj

58 **The oldest and most famous astronomical clock in the world is the Prague Astronomical Clock or Prague Orloj, fixed on the old town hall wall since 1410.** It displays not only the time but also the positions of the sun, moon, the major planets and zodiacal constellations. It has an astronomical dial, a mechanical clock and a calendar dial. Between 9 a.m. and 11 p.m., the moving figures of the 12 Apostles, along with others, appear on the hour at the small windows of the tower in the 'Walk of the Apostles'. Statues of various Catholic saints are on either side of the clock. Death is shown as a skeleton with an alleged ghost on top.

59 **Like the Bell Clock Tower, which is a gift to the city of Edinburgh from a local whisky distillery, clock towers have also been built as advertisements for private and government companies.**

60 **The tallest clock tower in the world today is the Makkah Royal Clock Tower, which is 1,972 ft high.** Across from Islam's most sacred Great Mosque of Mecca in Saudi Arabia is the country's largest skyscraper complete with malls, hotels and shops, the Abraj al-Abait. It has a four-sided clock, the Makkah Royal Clock Tower, modelled on the Westminster clock in London, has been up and running since 2010.

61 **If you are curious about the Resurrection of Christ, just drop in to see the Besancon Cathedral astronomical**

clock in France. Built in 1860, it has more than 30,000 parts to keep it going. Twenty-one automated figures and animated pictures indicate how the Resurrection of Christ led to the existence of man.

62 **The Rostock astronomical clock built in 1472 and set in St. Mary's Church in Rostock, Germany, has a calendar that was valid up to 2017.**

63 **Why should clocks be boring?** In Lier, Belgium, they are not. At the stroke of 12 noon, the Belgian coat of arms, the first three kings of Belgium, Lier's coat of arms, the jubilee years 1830–1930, and the six mayors who have governed Lier since Belgium's independence, all pop out of the clock to tell you the time. This Belgian Jubilee clock developed by Louis Zimmer in 1930 and installed on the Zimmer Tower to celebrate the 100th year of Belgium's independence, still works on the hour.

64 **Bell-ringing shepherds and trumpet-blowing angels mark the procession of the Magi in the St. Mark's Clock in the Piazza San Marco in Venice.** Built in 1497, the clock displays the time, the phase of the moon and zodiac positions. Two bronze figures atop the tower strike the bell hourly. On special days, carved figures of the four Magi join the two bronze figures said to be Moors. They come out from the clock face and bow to the figure of the Virgin Mary above. An angel blows a trumpet and the Magi bow in return!

St. Mark's Clock

65 Diamond Jubilee Tower Clocks were built all over the UK to commemorate and celebrate Queen Victoria's long reign.

66 **Glockenspiel clocks are tiny automated theatres.** Glockenspiel, meaning 'bell play in German, is a percussion instrument similar to a xylophone. These bells were later replaced by steel bars like the xylophone. Glockenspiel clocks, seen on many clock towers around the world, are custom-made and use moving figurines that, at different times of the day, put up a mechanized play or skit that is important to a town's history.

67 **Big Ben is the name of the four faced bell inside the tower and not the tower itself.** One of the most famous clocks of all time, the Big Ben stands spectacularly prominent in London. It took 13 years to build and chimes every 15 minutes on the dot. Built in 1858, it was placed in the Elizabeth Tower attached to the Palace of Westminster, the UK parliament in London, on the banks of the river Thames.

68 **Why the name 'Big Ben?** Nobody really knows but it could be after Sir Benjamin Hall, the first commissioner for works who was responsible for commissioning it. It is 7 ft 2 inches high, with an 8 ft 10 inch diameter and 334 steps. How much do two big African elephants weigh? Well, the Big Ben weighs exactly that – about 13.5 tonnes.

69 **Every time Big Ben chimes it rings out the musical note 'E'. And the four bells inside striking G sharp, F sharp and E sharp notes ring in the quarter-hours. Believe**

70 **A clock tower hosts a whole show in Munich, Germany.** Watch 32 life-sized costumed figures enact a royal wedding, a jousting tournament and some lovely dancing, all based on Munich's popular folklore, complete with 43 ringing bells playing different tunes. This 12–15 minute spectacle is put on by the Rathaus-Glockenspiel clock tower at 11a.m. and mid-day (and 5 p.m. between March and October) every day and ends with a golden cuckoo up on top, popping out to chirp three times.

it or not, the Big Ben has a tilt! The top of the clock tower is leaning 1.5 ft off a level position. 'O Lord, keep safe our Queen Victoria the First' in Latin is imprinted on its face.

71 **Among the famous clock towers in the world is India's own Rajabai Clock Tower in Mumbai.** The British loved to build clock towers, so every city, big or small, boasts of one *Ghanta Ghar* or the other. At the Fort campus of the University of Mumbai, the Rajabai clock tower stands tall at 280 ft. Designed by Sir George Gilbert Scott, an English architect who modelled it on the Big Ben, the Rajabai Clock Tower used to play many tunes. It currently chimes only one tune every 15 minutes.

Rajabai Clock Tower

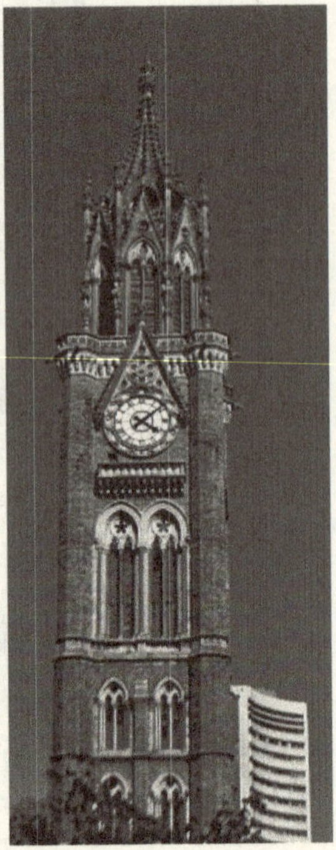

72 **Even before the British came to India, the Jantar Mantar in Jaipur and Delhi were hailed as Raja Jai Singh's contribution to discovering planetary positions and 'time'.** It has some remarkable concrete astronomical instruments that not only give time using the 43 ft sundial, but also help to fix the distances of planets, celestial altitudes and related data.

73 **Believe it or not, a clock tower was a prison.** Switzerland has the 13th century Zytglogge Tower in Bern, that often doubled as a prison and a guard tower. It became a clock tower in the 15th century and has two faces that represent the sky at different hours. It also has a Julian calendar dial and zodiac details.

5

FORTS

A fort is different from a castle in that it is not a residence, but rather a military fortification. These structures have been built specifically with war in mind and used to defend specific territories.

74 **While palaces are ornate and lavish royal residences, castles are fortified residences of noblemen and forts are functional military establishments that have troops stationed there.** Forts were designed to defend large territories or cities and not just the nobleman or village. Different kinds of forts – bastion, star and polygonal – were built to combat superior artillery fire once gunpowder was invented.

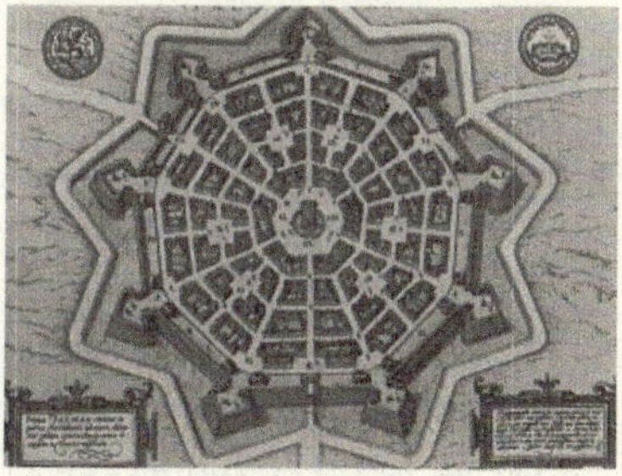

A star fort

75 **Built in the 16th century by King Philip II, the Citadel of Jaca in Spain was one of the world's earliest bastion forts.** The ground plan was pentagonal, with five reinforced bastions or projections armed with cannons at each corner. It had a moat, covered walkways, an open parade ground and an external downward slope. There were five barracks to accommodate 300 troops.

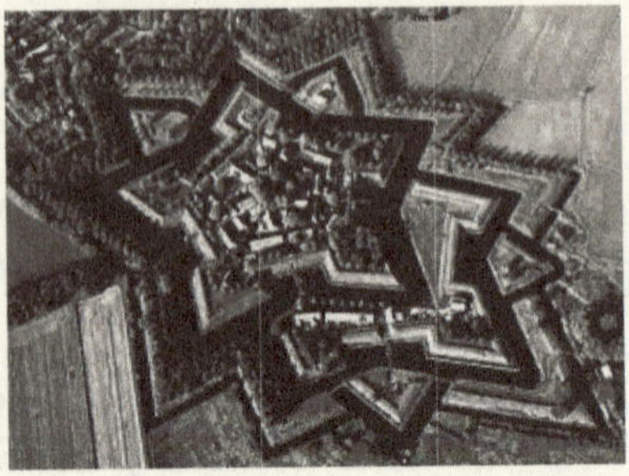
Fort Bourtange

76 **Fort Bourtange in the Netherlands is one of the most well-preserved examples of a star fort.** It is a bastion fort consisting of many triangular bastions designed to cover each other and the ditch. It provided covering fire from many angles and was a very flat structure with low thick brick walls because brick, unlike stone does not shatter on being hit by cannonballs. Built in 1,593, William of Orange, it was converted from a fort to a village in 1851.

77 **'Castrametation' is the art of setting up a military camp or constructing a fortification.**

78 **A prominent landmark in New York Harbor, Castle Williams is a circular fortification of red sandstone on the northwest point of Governors Island, USA.** A polygonal fort, it was designed in early 19th century to protect New York City from naval attacks. It is a fortress with no bastions but arranged in rings around the area that needed to be protected. Each ring could support the other. Very adaptable and capable of thwarting artillery fire, polygonal forts were quite popular with the military and were built right up to the 20th century.

79 **Inhabited since the 3rd century BCE, Citadel of Aleppo in the old city of Aleppo, Syria, is the oldest and largest ancient fortress in the world.** Spread over 428,446 sq. ft and surrounded by a moat, it has an amphitheatre,

Turkish baths and many underground tunnels and caves. During the 'Battle of Aleppo' in the civil war in Syria in 2015, the citadel was damaged badly.

80 **Janjira in is a massive sea fort on an island near Murud in Maharashtra, India.** Built in 1736 by the Abyssinian minister of the sultan of Ahmednagar, the fortress could easily take on around 572 cannons. Only approachable by the sea, it is famously the only fort in India that has never ever been captured. Undefeated despite many massive hostile attempts, its 19 bastions and most of its fortifications are intact.

81 **Built by Rao Jodha in 1460, Mehrangarh Fort in Jodhpur, India, is spread over 5 km.** A magnificent red sandstone structure, it rises 410 ft above the city. Chiselled from the rock on which it stands, the building

Mehrangarh Fort

appears to merge with its base. Expanded by Maharaja Ajit Singh in the 17th century, it is enclosed by imposing thick walls with battlements that are 19.6 ft to 118 ft high. Seven massive gates, some with iron spikes – to deter elephants – are still intact, despite the marks of some 1,800 cannonball hits.

82 **Gibraltar, famous for 'The Rock of Gibraltar', a stunning 1,397 ft high limestone rock rising out of the sea, is also the world's only natural fortress.** In 1309, King Fernando IV of Castile defeated the Moors and occupied Gibraltar. A very narrow peninsula at the southern edge of Spain, it overlooks the Strait of Gibraltar and the northern coastal areas of Africa. It is also the entry point to the Mediterranean. So, realizing its importance, he built a keep or tower there and a dockyard for his galleys, and turned it into a fortress.

83 **Spain lost Gibraltar to Britain in a battle in1713 and it became a British Crown colony in 1830 and remains one to date.** With its fortifications clustered in three main areas, it has a tunnel network inside the Rock that is about 52 km long and includes an underground telephone exchange, a power-generating station, a water distillation plant, a hospital, a bakery, a vehicle maintenance workshop and more.

84 **The Kremlin (meaning 'fortress') in Russia is an impressive red and green fort complex on the river Moskva in the heart of Moscow.** The site was occupied since the 2nd century BCE. Built up from a fortified structure – in the 12th century – by Prince Yuri Dolgoruky, who founded Moscow, it was first made of oak wood, then turned to stone and finally

into brick. It was the most powerful fortress in Russia. It is spread over 90 acres, and surrounded by walls 201 km long. It has five palaces, four cathedrals, the Kremlin Wall and 20 Kremlin towers, of which the tallest, Troitskaya, is 80 ft high. The Tsar Bell, the largest in the world, has never rung

85 **Ranikot Fort in Pakistan, now under restoration, is believed to be the world's largest fort, with a** circumference of 32 km. Its limestone ramparts are as impressive as those of the Great Wall of China. It connects several peaks of the Kirthar Mountains. There is a smaller fort within, called the Miri Fort, which is about 3 km from the main gate and was the palace of the Mir royal family. A zigzag fort, it has four entry gates in the shape of a diamond.

86 **There are more than 40,000 'Ring Forts' in Ireland.** They are nothing more than farmhouses surrounded by huge mounds of earth or stone. However, there were said to be fairies living between the rings and the forts are said to be protected by magic!

87 **Fort St. George in Chennai, India, was built by the East India Company in 1644. It was the first British fortress in India and was named after England's patron saint, St. George.**

88 **Warwick Castle in Warwickshire built in 1068 by William the Conqueror is among the oldest fortified structures in England.** It houses a trebuchet, an old medieval launching siege weapon. It is a catapult about three storeys high, which can launch a 13 kilo missile about 800 ft away at a speed of 25 kmph. It is demonstrated on certain days.

89 **Malbork Castle or Marienburg in Poland is the world's largest brick-built castle–fort.** Spread over a mindboggling large 1,539,239 sq. ft, it was built in 1406 during the Crusades. Developed from a simple convent into a massive fort with deep moats, heavy walls, cannon bases and many buildings, it is now a museum.

90 **The hexagonal Pallippuram Fort in Vyppin in Kerala, India, was built by the Portuguese in 1503 and is the oldest surviving European fort in India. Captured by the Dutch in 1661, it was sold to the Travancore Maharaja in 1789.**

91 **One of the oldest fort structures are the ruins of ancient fortifications at Sisupalgarh in Odisha, India.** It is dated to the 3rd century BCE and was occupied for at least 1,000 years. It is estimated that it had eight gates, thick walls and possibly a deep moat around it.

92 **The Cheyenne Mountain Complex, an underground bunker (North American Aerospace Defense Command), is a 20th-century fortress built deep into a mountain in El Paso County, Colorado, USA.** Built in 1961 under 1968.5 ft of granite, over an area of 5 acres, it contains 15 facilities that are earthquake and explosion proof. Each is three storeys high and sits on a bed of about 1,000 giant springs designed to prevent them from moving more than an inch.

93 **Spread over an area of 256 acres, the Red Fort in Delhi, India, took ten years to build.** This grand structure was constructed by Mughal Emperor Shah Jahan when he shifted his capital from Agra to Delhi in 1638. This impressively grand fort took ten years to build. It was here that the last Mughal Emperor was tried

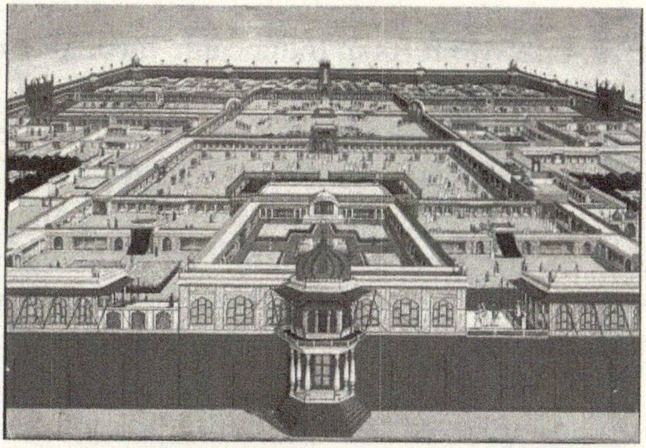

View of Red Fort (1785)

for treason and exiled to Burma. It was also here from its ramparts that India's first prime minister, Jawaharlal Nehru, hoisted the national flag in independent India in 1947, a tradition that continues on 15 August.

94 **The famous Red Fort in Delhi was originally largely white.** The fortification walls were made of red sandstone, but the buildings used a traditional white 'Mughal plaster' made from ground marble, dhal pulses, lime and fruit juice and were painted red in the mid-19th century. When the white stone started chipping off, the building was painted red by the British.

95 **India has more than 1,000 large forts.** The Chittorgarh Fort in Rajasthan is one of the largest. Built on a hill 590.6 ft high and spread over 691.9 acres, this fort (where the hauntingly beautiful Rani Padmini is said to have lived) is shaped like a fish. It has four palace complexes, nineteen main temples, four memorials and 20 ponds among its 64 in-house structures.

96 **Water supply to forts in India came through a unique system of *baolis*. These are step-wells, in which earthen pipes brought up the water. One such step-well built thousands of years ago in the 9th century is Chandi Baoli in Abhaneri in Rajasthan. It is one of the largest and most architecturally stunning *baolis* in India. The 3,500 small steps built in absolute symmetry take you 65 ft down to the well.**

97 The Arthashastra, an Indian treatise on political, economic and military strategy, describes six major types of forts:
* ***Jal durg***: A fortress surrounded by water, with two sub-types: the island fortress, and the 'plain' one, surrounded by artificial moats filled with water.
* ***Giri durg***: A hill or mountain fortress, with three types: one built on the summit of a hill or a mountain; the second one, where both major fortifications and other non-military structures are built down the mountain/hill slope besides including the summit; and third in which the living quarters are located in a valley surrounded by high hills, which have outposts and defensive walls.
* ***Vana durg***: A fort surrounded by dense forest of at least 4 *kroshas* (14.6 km). One type was built on a kind of mire and surrounded by thorny vegetation, and the other was built in a jungle.
* ***Dhanu durg***: These desert or waterless fortresses were built in barren, dry areas.
* ***Mahi durg***: This 'earth' fortress was protected by walls or quicksand.
* ***Nar durg***: This 'fortress with men' had a massive army to protect it.

6

HOMES

A home is where you make it. It could be a tent or a trailer, but over the course of history more and more people in the world have moved to homes with walls and a roof. Such homes could range from a hut to a seven-bedroom penthouse on the hundredth floor of a skyscraper.

98 **Houses of the Harappan Civilization (c. 3300–c. 1300 BCE), spread over a large area of north-west India and present-day Pakistan, were simple architecturally but amazing for the time.** People lived in houses that were 2–3 storeys high and made of mud bricks/sun-dried bricks and, in later stages, of baked bricks. All houses sewage systems made with mud bricks and ran under the street. The bathroom was a small square or rectangular room with a pavement inclined towards a corner, with an outlet for water. All houses in a town were identical, and built together in courtyards. Connecting the upper levels to lower ones were sets of brick stairs or sometimes ladders.

Harappan house

Some houses, probably those of the poorer people, did not have a roof.

99 **The Pygmies of the Congo Ituri rainforests, even today, need to move every few weeks in a nomadic lifestyle and build their homes quickly and resourcefully.** Using readily available leaves and saplings, they build their beehive shaped dome huts in a matter of hours. When chasing or hunting forest antelopes, buffalos and other means of food, such homes come in handy.

100 **Every time they move – at least twice a year – the Qashgai nomads of Iran carry their black desert tent homes with them, while herding their flock of goats and sheep.** Made of black goat wool, these tents are easily dismantled.

101 **The nomadic Eskimos or Inuits of Greenland, Alaska and Canada used to live in igloos, which are now mostly hunting lodges.** These are made of compacted snow on the inside. Many Inuit people used snow to insulate their houses constructed from whalebone and hides. In summer they lived in 'tupiqs' – tents made of caribou and seal skin.

102 **The havelis of northern and western India are elaborately decorated traditional homes with exteriors made of sandstone, marble or wood.** With rooms on different floors built around a central courtyard, they are usually large and are still around in their original form. Havelis of the Shekhawati region in Rajasthan, for instance, boast of exquisite frescos, paintings and murals influenced by Mughal art forms and Hindu mythology.

Facade of a haveli

103 **Mongolian nomadic tribes lived in 'yurts'.** Circular homes with animal-skin-covered collapsible wooden frames on thick canvas, they were cool in summer and warm in sub-zero conditions. On the move, the Mongolians simply used pack animals to carry them.

104 **Ancient Egyptians used the papyrus plant reed that grew in marshy lands to make their huts.** This was before they discovered that Nile river mud mixed with straw and sun dried made strong bricks. Egypt had no forests so wood was scarce and very rarely used. Instead they put the limestone they found nearby to good use.

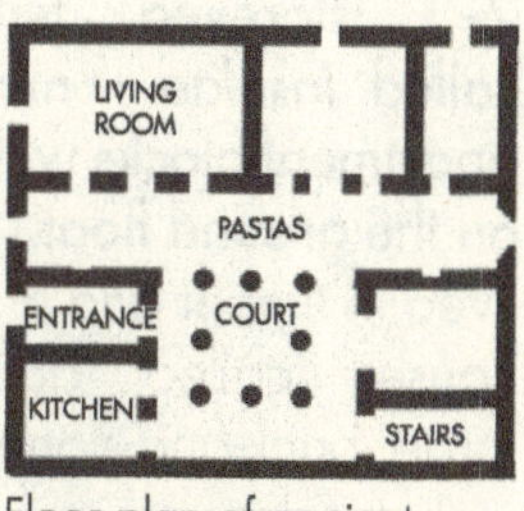

Floor plan of ancient Greek houses

1 **Early Greeks lived around open courtyards, made with tiled and decorated sun-baked**

mud bricks, that had pretty flowering plants and fruit-laden trees. With shuttered wooden windows built high to keep cool in summer and warm in winter, they could draw water from a well or pray at an altar to their gods or even play with a ball in the central area.

106 **The majority of early Greek and ancient Roman homes had no bathrooms.** They had to go to 'public baths' if they needed a wash. But these baths were not ordinary at all. In Rome, the public baths had hot and cold pools, towels, steam rooms, saunas, exercise rooms and hair-cutting salons. They even had reading rooms and libraries. It was a 'go to' place for friends to hang out. At one stage, Rome had 952 such communal baths. But the Greeks limited it to only hip baths and made do with bucket baths or a nearby stream or spring.

The entrance to a Roman villa

107 **In ancient Rome, the poor and the middle-class people lived in 2–3 storeyed tenements called *insulae* – mud-brick apartment blocks with shops on the ground floor.** The rich lived in timber and mud-brick houses called *domus* or large brick-and-stone 'villas' with gardens.

108 **Turf houses have been uniquely specific to Iceland.** Built on stone, they are made of solidified grass and dirt called 'sod', held together in a wooden frame and an ornate door. They look pretty with all that green turf sprouting on the roof but are no longer popular.

109 **Stilt houses are very popular in South East Asia.** With sloping roofs and planks, Cambodian and Vietnamese houses, for example, are built on stilts, designed so for protection from the incessant rains and consequent flooding, which bring in snakes, scorpions and other creepy-crawlies.

110 **In Cooper Pedy in Australia, there are underground houses dug deep into the earth.** Communities living there to escape the blisteringly hot sun of the outback also have an underground church and hotel. Rooms are ventilated through narrow vertical shafts. The top of those shafts poke out of the hills everywhere.

A chalet

111 **Popular in the snowy Alpine regions of Europe, especially Switzerland are the chalets. They are made of wood with heavy but gently sloping roofs that can take the weight of the snow.**

112 **Izbas are Russian traditional houses made of wooden logs and clay.** They have animal-skin-covered openings below the roof,

instead of windows, to keep out the biting cold. They were once very popular all over rural Russia.

113 **Traditional Chinese homes are called 'siheyuans'.** 'Si' stands for the directions – north, south, east and west. The south-east corner entrances are guarded by two lion statues and they have courtyards surrounded by blocks of living space. Once found everywhere, they are no longer as common.

114 **A 'rondavel' is a round hut made of stone topped by a thatched roof in South Africa.** It can withstand extreme weather conditions. It also helped save on space and energy and the general structure pattern of building is still being followed today.

Rondavels

115 **The Japanese 'minkas' have wooden verandahs running around them, with sliding doors.** They use tatami mat flooring, with an entrance hall to leave your shoes out. They are today considered 'cottages of old Japan'.

116 **The Japanese have designed an earthquake-proof house for protection against frequent earthquakes.** The house gently floats off its foundation about 1.1.8 inches in the air during an earthquake. It uses air pressure to levitate and then place itself back.

117 **Traditionally, people in Kerala, India, lived in *nallu kettus* – which consisted of four blocks of houses around a courtyard.** Simple and spacious living quarters, and specific to Kerala, they are around as ancestral homes.

A traditional *nallu kettu*

118 **Taking an average global three-person household as the base and coupling it with an 8 per cent population rise over the period points to the need for more than two billion new homes in the world by the end of the 21st century.**

119 **Home automation or 'domotics' (comes from the Latin word *domus*!) is all about building automation for a home, and such a home is called a smart home or smart house.** A home automation system will control lighting, temperatures, entertainment and other electronic systems and appliances, and security gadgets such as alarm systems for energy efficiency or convenience. Besides lights that come on according to daylight available, automated window shades and climate control, smart homes may also have connected feeders for pets, timers to water plants when needed, and much more.

120 **Designed by Jonathan Adler, a real life replica of Barbie's house is spread over 3,500 sq. ft in Malibu in California, USA.** This pink and red home has a lounge with a large circular sofa; a living room with a hair chandelier in blonde and brown, hair-tasselled lamps next to colourful chairs; giant rugs monogrammed with a B, an enormous bed, and, yes, a closet with about 50 pairs of pink and red shoes. It also has a sunburst mirror over the fireplace made up of Barbie dolls.

121 **The smallest house in the world is in Germany.** Designed by architect Van Bo Le-Mentzel over 10.7 sq. ft, it is made of wood. It can be used both vertically and horizontally. Weighing just 40 kilos, it has wheels, and can be moved easily, quickly and parked anywhere.

122 **Architect Terry Brown designed and built the Mushroom House in the shape a fancy toadstool.** It is an ornamental one-bedroom house in Cincinnati, Ohio, USA, with copper ceilings and a spiral staircase.

123 **The Slide House in Japan has three floors and no staircases. It has slides. You slide in and out of floors!**

124 **Liu Lingchao from China built himself a house that can be packed and carried!** It is made of plastic bags, bamboo and sheets, and weighs 59.8 kilos.

7

LIBRARIES

If you thought that libraries are just big rooms full of books, you are about to change your mind. Many library buildings have been and continue to be feats of brilliant and headlining architecture too.

125 **The early libraries consisted of archives of the earliest form of writing in 'Cuneiform' on clay tablets preserved in temple rooms.** As many as 30,000 clay tablets were recovered from the library of Ashurbanipal in Mesopotamia (now Iraq) stored in reed baskets and clay shelves.

126 **Built in the 3rd century, the world's first known library was the Library of Alexandria in Egypt.** Destroyed completely during the Roman conquest in 30 BCE, it has now been restored by the firm Snohetta in 2002. It is a circular building, 11 storeys high and with a tilting roof. Its facade is covered in characters from 100 different languages. The building itself tilts towards the sea like a sundial. It houses four museums and a planetarium as well.

Library of Alexandria

127 **Built in 859 CE, the oldest operating library in the world today is the Al-Qarawiyyin Library in Fez, Morocco.** It has 4,000 rarest of rare books, including a 10th century account of Prophet Mohammad's life.

128 **The Thomas Jefferson Building, once the Library of the US Congress, has the world's largest collection of comic books and books for children, and is also the world's largest library.** Marble columns, statues and busts of many famous thinkers and cultural figures decorate the ornamental exterior as well as the interior. Founded in 1880, its 883 miles (1,421 km) of shelves hold 33 million books, 68 million manuscripts, five million maps – the largest map collection in the world – and more than 6–13.5 million pieces of music and photographs.

Thomas Jefferson Building

129 **The 280-foot long Rococo-style Mafra Palace Library in Portugal, completed in 1775, has for centuries had a unique way of saving its 36,000 leather-bound volumes from havoc-wreaking pests.** While most libraries control pests, such as bookworms, moths and other insects, with chemicals or gamma radiation, this library, which has manuscripts dating from the 14th to the 19th centuries, uses an army of bats! During the day they stay behind the bookcases or out in the garden, and at night they hunt down the pests.

130 **The Library of Parliament in Ottawa, Canada, resembles a multicoloured Gothic castle.** Green and

Canadian Library of Parliament

purple slate strips and red sandstone give the facade its unusual look. It has some 16 flying buttresses or arches, a three-tiered roof topped by a cupola, plus many stone motifs and carvings that make this structure, built in 1876, look like medieval European libraries across the Atlantic!

131 **The eight-storey library of the Aberdeen University in Scotland has won awards for its bold, innovative architecture.** Irregular vertical stripes of insulated panels and glass form the outside, giving it a zebra-like look in contrast to the university's beginnings in 1495, while the inside is all full of easy curves around a single atrium. The library was completed in 2012. It has 13 km of shelves and more than a million books.

132 **The resemblance of the Trinity College Library in Dublin, Ireland, to the Jedi Temple archives in the 2002 Star Wars Episode II: *Attack of the Clones* is amazing.** Its 213 ft long room has carved dark wood pilasters – flat rectangular columns – and a remarkable barrel vault ceiling. Marble busts of writers, philosophers and philanthropists line the central hall. It was first opened in 1592 and has over six million volumes.

133 **American steel industrialist and philanthropist Andrew Carnegie (1835–1919) founded 2,509 libraries in the USA, UK, Australia and New Zealand. He is popularly known as the 'Patron Saint of Libraries'.**

134 **An odd-angled shining marble facade in polished 'absolute black' granite fronts the Royal Library in Copenhagen, Denmark, nicknamed the 'Black Diamond'.** The black cladding of 26,909 sq. ft is made up of stone blocks from Zimbabwe, each weighing 75 kg and polished in Italy. Built in 1999, this modern structure, which is an extension of the old 17th century library, is made up of two black cubes sliced by an atrium of clear glass that allows the sun to come shining through.

135 **The George Peabody Library, Baltimore, USA, with 300,000 volumes, is a wedding destination.** Designed and built by architect Edmund G. Lind in 1878, it has a gold columned five-tier central atrium with black and white marble floors. Sunlight streams through from its latticed skylight 61 ft above. Its balconies are in ornamental cast iron and the whole effect is grand.

George Peabody Library

136 **The National Library of Prague, Czech Republic, known as the 'Clementinum', was given a makeover in 1722.** The 18th century 223 ft high astronomical tower was once an observatory. With its collection of rare gilded globes and remarkable frescoes on the ceiling, the main library hall itself is a masterpiece of awe-inspiring Baroque architecture. It houses some six million documents including some in Greek papyri.

137 **A library that looks straight out of Harry Potter landscape, the Bibliotheque Sainte Genevieve in Paris, France, dates to 1851.** Designed in all metal by architect Henri Labrouste, its facade has some 700 names engraved on it. It has a striking barrel vaulted ceiling inside, with decorative cast-iron arches supported by iron pillars. With light streaming in through 46 large arched glass windows set high on its walls that are lined with books, and rows and rows of long desks below, it looks like a scene straight out of Hogwarts. Spread over 19,000 sq. ft, it houses books inherited from Sainte Genevieve, the oldest abbey in France, and some two million items.

138 **The columns of the 'Tower of the Five Orders', decorated in five architectural styles – the Tuscan, Doric, Ionic, Corinthian and Composite – form the main entrance to the Bodleian Library, UK.** Built in 1602, it is one of the oldest in the world and is part of a group of 28 Oxford University Library buildings. They say that every second someone uses its digital collection, every 14 seconds someone visits its libraries and every 21 seconds someone borrows a book. Its wood-panelled rooms house more than 13 million printed items.

139 **Designed by Dutch architect Rem Koolhaas, the Seattle Public Library's Central Library branch is a 21st century building in steel and glass squares.** Spread over 3,63,000 sq. ft, it has diagonal lattice panelling and cubes at unconventional angles that make it look like futuristic. It is 11 storeys high with a million books. Almost 4,000 tonnes of steel, which could build 20 Statues of Liberty and glass sheets that could cover maybe five and a half football fields, were used for it.

140 **At the Musashino Art University Museum and Library in Tokyo, Japan, the shelves are stacked not with books but with people.** It has huge bookcases the entire height of the wall, but many are without books. The people occupy the shelves as well!

141 **A fortress-like library, inspired by Nature and set among lush botanical gardens, is the Biblioteca Jose Vasconcelos in Mexico City, Mexico.** But inside, it has glass-and-steel box bookshelves that appear to hang in the air. Covering 4,09,000 sq. ft with 5,00,000 books, this 70 ft container-like structure is popularly called 'Megabiblioteca'. Designed by architect Alberto Kalach, it houses a large skeleton sculpture of a whale in the lobby.

142 **The Stuttgart City Library in Germany will remind you of the Rubik's cube.** With a cuboid facade of frosted glass blocks set in pale grey concrete, it is crystal white during the day but at night radiates bright blue light. On the inside, it is like an amazing inverted ziggurat or step pyramid, with neatly aligned almost-spiral stairways. Bright and white, it also has a fountain in the centre. Its pristine white walls lined with books are eye-catching, but its main attraction is its five-story open atrium that appears to merge with the glass roof. Designed by Yi Architects in 2011, it is considered a modern architectural wonder.

143 **An unusual place to be in, but the Austrian National Library is inside one of Europe's more spectacular palaces.** The Hofburg Palace in Vienna is not only the home to the country's president, but also to some 7.4 million books. Two storeys of carved wooden galleries filled with more than 200,000 rare leather-bound books

144 **Norway's Vennesla Library and Culture House's rib concept is incredible.** Under a single curved roof, but entirely made up of 27 prefabricated timber and plywood ribs that create cushioned reading niches and built-in shelves, it is unique. The wooden ribs appear to bend around walls and the ceiling seamlessly along with its lighting, bookshelves and seating before merging with the floor. Built in 2011, its interior reminds one of a futuristic airplane.

line the sides, and wooden staircases on wheels criss-cross the book walls. It also has some magnificent frescoes by painter Daniel Gran, on the ceiling. It was established in1368 as an Imperial Court Library.

145 **The ancient university and library of Nalanda in India was destroyed in 1193 by Bakhtiyar Khilji,**

who hoped to uproot Buddhism. And with it were destroyed many ancient Indian scientific treatises in mathematics, astronomy, alchemy and anatomy that were stored in the library. The ruins still exist.

146 **The Harvard University Library has a book, *Des Destinees de l'Ame* (Destinies of the Soul), bound in – you will never guess what – human skin!**

147 **The Los Angeles Public Library has a combination of many architectural styles, including a mosaic pyramid.** Inside, brilliant murals on the walls and the ceiling depict the history of California. A chandelier, with a stained-glass globe and zodiac symbols surrounding it, with a ring of 48 small lights depicting the 48 states of the USA, hangs in the centre. There is also a seven-foot statue of a female figure holding a book and keeping company with two sphinxes. Built in 1912, it also has a huge children's literature section.

148 **The Beinecke Rare Book & Manuscript Library at Yale University has no windows.** That's because the walls are made of translucent marble–granite, glass and bronze, which let the light filter in. It houses a Gutenberg Bible, the first book ever printed.

149 **The Library of Celsus in Turkey is also a tomb!** It was built from 114–117 CE as a mausoleum for the Roman senator Tiberius Julius Celsus Polemaeanus, governor of the province of Asia, who was buried below the library with a statue of Athena – the goddess of wisdom – above it. In its heyday, it contained more than 12,000 parchments and was one of the largest libraries in the world. Today, only its facade remains.

8

LIGHTHOUSES

Since ancient times, seafarers have navigated their way through storms, shifting whirlpools, icebergs, rocks and other dangers. Stars in the sky, a volcanic fire here or a cloud formation there helped them find their way. Lighthouses were one way to stop them crashing into rocks.

150 **Lighthouses first burnt wood for light.** Gradually oil lamps took over. Whale oil was often used as fuel. In 1782, Swiss scientist Aimé Argand invented the Argand lamp, an oil lamp that emitted a steady smokeless flame and it revolutionized lighthouse illumination. Today, however, lighthouses are electronically lit and operated. If visibility is poor, automatic sensors turn on the fog signals and radio signals communicate with the ships. The fog horn sounds the warning to stay clear.

151 **The oldest known lighthouse, the Pharos of Alexandria, was one of the ancient wonders of the world.** In ancient Alexandria, the Egyptians tired of rescuing shipwrecked sailors washing up on their rocky shores, and built the Lighthouse of Alexandria in 12 years from

Lighthouse of Alexandria, drawing (1909)

280 to 247 BCE. A marble tower rising 450 ft high, it lasted many centuries and survived many earthquakes. For almost 1,500 years it warned ships. Its light was said to be visible 465 km out into the sea. It had 300 rooms for the lighthouse keepers and the staff. Finally, a massive earthquake in the 5th century destroyed it. Using some of its stones, a fort now stands on the platform that it once stood on.

152 **Pharos is the Greek word for Lighthouse. The study of lighthouses is called 'pharology' and those who study lighthouses are called 'pharologists'.**

153 **The rotating beams of lighthouses, known as a 'beacon', warn ships about their whereabouts and help as a navigational aid. It is like a traffic signal in the open seas. The higher and taller it is, the farther its beam is likely to travel.**

154 **The Tower of Hercules is the oldest functioning lighthouse in Spain, a UNESCO world heritage site, and the oldest Roman lighthouse in use today.** After three nights of heavy fighting, it is said, Hercules the Great cut off the head of his enemy giant Geryon and buried him. He built a city above it and called it Corunna. Whether it's true or not, the lighthouse is seen atop a skull and crossbones (representing the buried head of Geryon!) in the coat of arms of the city of Corunna. With 242 steps to the top, the lighthouse is about 180 ft tall on a 187 ft high rock and overlooks the North Atlantic coast of Spain.

Corunna coat-of-arms with a lighthouse

155 There are officially more than 20,700 lighthouses in the world, according to the Lighthouse Directory.

156 The first lighthouse in England, the Eddystone Lighthouse, was built near Rame Head in 1698. However, it was destroyed twice. In 1759, English engineer John Smeaton rebuilt it. Using granite blocks, he designed it like an oak tree. Built from interlocking blocks of stone instead of wood, which strengthened the structure to withstand powerful waves, it became a model for later lighthouses.

157 The only light house with a helipad (on its rooftop) is the Eddystone Lighthouse. It is 12 nautical miles off the shore of England.

158 In 1822, Augustine Fresnel of France discovered something of great use to lighthouses. It was the 'Fresnel lens', which captured and focused 85 per cent of the light that was emitted. It beamed better, brighter and longer so that ships could spot rotating flashes more easily. The lens was used by later lighthouses.

Torch of the Statue of Liberty

159 The Statue of Liberty was not just a huge statue gifted to the Americans by the French to commemorate their independence in 1886. It was a lighthouse too. At 326 ft high, it warned ships to steer away from the rocky shores near the New York harbour. Frederic Bartholdi, the French sculptor, had planned to place

floodlights on the balcony around the statue's torch, but that idea was rejected for fear that the light would blind the pilots of the passing ships. Subsequently, portholes were cut into the torch, the lights placed inside and the torch covered with gold leaf. It was the first lighthouse to install electric lights and its beams could be seen around 38.5 km away, till its torch was deactivated in 1902.

160 **The first American lighthouse, built in 1716, was on Little Brewster Island at the entrance to the Boston harbour.** This is where the Americans threw out all that British tea at what is now famous as the Boston Tea Party and the British blew it up during the American War of Independence in 1776. Rebuilt in 1783, this lighthouse, the Boston Light, is the only 'manned' one in the USA today.

161 **At the Jeddah Seaport in Saudi Arabia is the tallest lighthouse in the world.** The 436 ft high Jeddah Light is not only an ultra-modern lighthouse but it is also Jeddah's port and harbour control room. It has a range of 46 km and emits three white flashes every 20 seconds.

162 **The USA has the highest number of lighthouses in the world. It has more than 1,000 of them spread all over the country.**

163 **A lighthouse on a mountain pass is not what you would expect to see.** Yet there is one in the Surselva region of Graubunden canton, Switzerland. The lighthouse, built above the longest rail tunnel in the world in the Alps, at 6712 ft above sea level, is the highest in the world.

164 **Among the oldest in the world and the oldest in Ireland, the 3rd century Hook Lighthouse was manned by**

monks. When ships failed to safely navigate the Waterford harbour in Ireland, a Welsh monk set about burning wood and timber atop piles of stones to warn them that land was near. The lighthouse now functions as an automated one.

165 **Built in 1962, the newest lighthouse in the USA is Charleston Light on Sullivans Island, South Carolina. This triangular lighthouse is the only one in the USA with an elevator and air-conditioning.**

166 **A lighthouse is disappearing!** On a cliff once 60 m above sea level among the shifting sand dunes of Jutland's North Sea coast is the Rubjerg Knude Lighthouse, built in 1899. With the sea winds churning up sand towards the lighthouse and causing the sands to move and bury, the structure of the lighthouse seems to be disappearing among the sands. It is expected to fall into the sea by 2023.

167 **A lighthouse in Germany can tell you the time.** Built in 1856, the 108 ft Lindau Lighthouse on Lake Constance has a massive clock visible all over the city and a lighthouse that used to be lit by a fire.

168 **The Ponta Bonita lighthouse in the Marin Headlands, an hour's drive from San Francisco in California, USA, has a detailed record of 300 shipwrecks on its rocks.**

169 **Lighthouses are painted white, or red and white to enable ships to identify them.** They also have different flash patterns from one another to indicate where they are to mariners who have lost their bearings.

170 **The oldest active lighthouse in the USA is the Sandy Hook Light at Gateway National Recreation Area in Fort Hancock, New Jersey. It first lit the night in 1764.**

171 **Of course, there would be a lighthouse with a ghost story!** The South Stack Lighthouse on the Welsh coast is said to have a ghost on watch. In 1853, a frightening storm hit the Anglesey coast in Wales and wrecked almost 200 ships. The lighthouse keeper Jack Jones, who kept ships warned with 21 oil lamps, was also killed and it is believed he roams the area at night, especially during storms. Now the lighthouse is fully automated.

9

MAUSOLEUMS AND TOMBS

Tributes to famous dead people express the feelings of those building them in many architecturally wonderful ways. They often also reflect the beliefs and convictions of those buried there.

172 **The term 'mausoleum' comes from the name of King Mausolus of Caria, a satrap of the Achaemenid Empire, whose mausoleum is known as the Tomb of Mausolus or the Mausoleum of Halicarnassus.** Grand and elaborate, it was one of the earliest wonders of the world.

173 **The Mausoleum of Halicarnassus near Bodrum in Turkey was designed by Greek architects Satyros and Pytheos, and built atop a hill between 353 and 350 BCE.** Made of white marble with a courtyard around it, it had on top an enormous statue of Mausolus and his wife Artemisia in a chariot pulled by four horses. This 4th century BCE edifice was 140 ft high, with a base 120 ft by 100 ft, and rested on elegant Greek Ionic columns. Stone soldiers on horsebacks corners guarded the king and his queen said to be buried below. Pliny the Elder's

writings describe in detail its beauty and workmanship, though it was destroyed by earthquakes.

174 **The 'Pyramid of Giza' near Cairo, Egypt, is the final resting place of the Egyptian pharaoh Khufu or Cheops.** Built in 2560 BCE and about 50 storeys high (481 ft), it was the tallest structure in the world for the next 3,800 years. At the base it is almost a perfect square. Looted of almost everything except for Khufu's red-granite sarcophagus or mummified remains, the three huge chambers inside are said to have once been brimming with treasures. Next to it is buried an enormous ship 147.6 ft long, perhaps to ferry the pharaoh to heaven....

175 **How was the Giza/Khufu Pyramid built at a time when precision tools, cranes, elevators or modern winches were unknown?** It took the Egyptians 2.3 million blocks of stone and 20 years to complete it. So with nothing but wood, rope and animals, they must have carted 800 tonnes of stone a day, from quarries far away, on crude wooden sleds, then pulled them up mud ramps

The Sphinx and the Pyramid of Giza

and painstakingly put each stone in place one by one. Some blocks apparently weighed more than 9 tonnes.

176 **Just like the Egyptians, the Chinese are also known for being buried with their treasures for a good afterlife.** Enormous mausoleums line the Chinese Cemetery of Manila in the Philippines, They come with fully functioning kitchens, bathrooms with luxury fittings and plush bedrooms for relatives who visit the dead, light incense sticks and stay on too.

177 **Jade and crystal from China, lapis lazuli from Afghanistan, turquoise from Tibet, jasper from Punjab, sapphire from Sri Lanka and carnelian from Arabia – all in all, 28 types of precious and semi-precious stones were inlaid into the lustrous white Makrana marble that went into the making of the famous Taj Mahal in Agra, India, built between 1632 and 1653.**

178 **Some 22,000 workers and artisans are said to have laboured over 21 years to raise the great tribute of**

Taj Mahal

Mughal Emperor Shah Jahan to his third wife Mumtaz Mahal. Working on the Taj Mahal were sculptors, calligraphists and stone cutters from as far away as Bukhara, Syria and Baluchistan.

179 **With a spectacular marble clad dome, 115 ft high, surrounded by four smaller domes, all framed by four minarets at the corners, the Taj Mahal is set in a 42-acre garden.** It has Quranic verses, floral designs and lattice work on its exteriors. The towers tilt away a little to prevent them from falling in and damaging the tomb itself in the event of an earthquake.

180 **The Taj Mahal changes colour at different times of the day. If it's pink at dawn, it turns a lovely white at dusk and takes on a golden glow at night.**

181 **The mausoleum of Vladimir Lenin, leader of the Russian Revolution of 1917, is unique.** It is in a majestic building, designed by A.V. Shchusev, on Moscow's Red Square. Lenin's embalmed body lies since 1924 under a lit glass canopy, over which is thrown a crepe covering of mighty proportions. Kept at a temperature of 16°C and humidity levels of 80–90 per cent, it is moisturized daily and injected with preservatives to keep it intact. Every 18 months it undergoes a special chemical bath. A 'mausoleum group' of five to six anatomists, biochemists and surgeons, is responsible for its maintenance. In red and black marble, porphyry, granite and labradorite, the mausoleum features a black one-piece 60-tonne slab with the lone inscription 'LENIN'.

Mausoleum of Lenin

182 **Famous for its chapel-like tombs, the Jardines Del Humaya Cemetery in Culiacan, Mexico, is a burial ground with a difference.** For visiting family and friends to grieve in comfort, these mausoleums have air-conditioning, living rooms, bedrooms, fully equipped kitchens, bulletproof glass, alarm systems and Wi-Fi.

183 **UK's largest private mausoleum in South Lanarkshire, Scotland, the Hamilton Mausoleum, is famous for its echo.** If a door slams shut, it takes 15 seconds for the sound to fade – which is a record. It was built by Alexander, the tenth Duke of Hamilton, as his final resting place. Grand and breathtaking with its massive dome, magnificent bronze doors, marble floors and the treasures inside, it has often been compared in riches to the Pyramids.

184 **The mausoleum of the first emperor of the 3rd century Qin Dynasty, Qin Shi Huang, famous for unifying China, is yet to be excavated, but the area in Xi'an showed up a startling find in 1974.** They discovered life-size terracotta figures of about 8,000 soldiers, 130 chariots with 520 horses and 150 cavalry horses lying in three deep pits. In lacquer finish, they were almost lifelike, with clear delineated features. Other treasures were also found – chariots, cranes, swans, ducks with groups of musicians in bronze plus the skeletons of all those labourers who worked on it. The rest of the necropolis or burial ground is yet to be excavated.

185 **Lampa in Peru is famous for the rather bizarre tomb of politician Enrique Torres Belon.** He designed his own tomb with hanging human skeletons and hundreds of skulls dug up from the town's cemetery and the tombs

beneath the church to which it is attached. It has a black marble cross at the bottom and on its dome is an aluminum replica of the Pieta – Michelangelo's famous sculpture of the body of Jesus on the lap of his mother Mary after the Crucifixion.

186 **In Uzbekistan, the mausoleum of Shah-i-Zinda (The Living King) is part of a whole avenue of mausoleums with many magnificent tombs.** This historic complex in Samarkand has a fascinating mix of architectural styles, with stunning tile work and mosaics. The monument is connected with the legend of Kusam ibn Abbas. It is believed that he was beheaded for his faith and later he took his head and went into the deep well here, and continues to live.

187 **Designed by Persian architect Mirak Mirza Ghiyath, Mughal Emperor Humayun's Tomb in Delhi is the world's first garden tomb.** Commissioned by Humayun's wife, it took eight years to build in 1570. The tomb graces the centre of a well-laid 30-acre 'Char Bagh' or the four-quadrant garden. Its white double marble dome, 154 ft high and flanked by glazed ceramic tiled *chhatris*, is also a first in India. Its design is said to be the inspiration for the Taj Mahal built about 60 years later.

Humayun's Tomb

188 **Humayun's Tomb is known as the 'dormitory of the Mughals' because there are about 150 more graves in the complex. One of these is Nai Ka Gumbad, the tomb of the royal barber.**

189 **The burial spirit houses of Alaska are unique and the size of doll's houses.** In some communities here, the body is buried and a blanket is placed over the grave. After 40 days, a little wooden 'spirit box', like a long doll's house painted in the family colours, is placed over the grave, and allowed to decay into the soil.

190 **Located on the periphery of Lahore, Pakistan, is the tomb of Mughal Emperor Jahangir, who was buried here in 1627. Quiet on the outside, its interiors are richly decorated with frescoes.**

191 **On the 'Hill of Calvary' or Golgotha, within the Church of the Holy Sepulchre in Jerusalem, Israel, is the Tomb of Jesus Christ.** This simple structure was built by Emperor Constantine's mother Helena in 330 CE, and commemorates the hill of crucifixion and the tomb of Christ's burial. Destroyed by the Persians in 614 CE, rebuilt again and then sacked by the Egyptian caliph al-Hakim in 1009 CE, it was finally reconstructed by the Crusaders.

192 **Inside the Church of the Holy Sepulchre, down some steps, is a large rocky cave-like area that indicates where Jesus was crucified.** Here is the two-chambered 'Edicule' or little house where the tomb is located. A marble slab covers the rock bench on which the body of Jesus lay. The facade had some crusader designs, which are now in a museum, but the bell tower still exists. This church is part of a vast complex housing six churches and 20 chapels.

193 **Mazar-e-Quaid or the Jinnah Mausoleum in Karachi, Pakistan, was designed by a Mumbai-based Indian architect, Yahya Merchant.** The final resting place of

Muhammad Ali Jinnah, the founder of Pakistan, it is built in white marble with arched curves and copper grills on an elevated platform with rows of fountains (15 of them) and terraces leading up to it. It is surrounded by a 53-acre park.

194 **On the river Tiber, at the head of Rome's famous 'Bridge of Angels', stands the towering cylindrical resting place of the famous emperor, Hadrian.** Castel Sant'Angelo or the Mausoleum of Hadrian was built by Hadrian himself and his ashes placed here in 138 CE. It had a statue of Hadrian dressed as a sun god driving a four-horse chariot. Now it is a museum.

195 **The mausoleum of Genghis Khan, built between 1954 and 1956 by the Chinese government in Ordos City, Inner Mongolia, in the traditional Mongol style, contains no body. It is a cenotaph, where the coffin contains only headdresses and accessories, as the actual tomb of Genghis Khan is debated.**

196 **A tomb to heartbreak, styled with sculpted orchids, is the Rufina Cambaceres Mausoleum in the Recoleta Cemetery in Buenos Aires, Argentina.** A young Argentine woman, she went into a coma and was buried here in 1902. It is said that she was buried alive in a shocking mistake. Her mother then built this grand tomb with a life-sized statue of Rufina holding the door to her own tomb.

197 **In Upper Manhattan in New York City in the USA stands the Grant's Tomb or the General Grant National Memorial, the final resting place of former American president Ulysses S. Grant (1822–85) and his wife Julia. The largest such memorial in North America, it was completed in 1897 and is a tribute to this president who helped end the American Civil War.**

10

MEMORIALS AND MONUMENTS

People across nations and over the centuries have always liked to record historical events and commemorate their heroes by building all kind of stunning structures as lasting tributes to them.

198 A 'memorial' is a structure or a statue that is built to remember a dead person or a group of people who died in an important past event.

199 A monument is a structure, statue, or a building that is built to honour someone notable or a special event. It comes from the Greek '*mnemosynon*' and the Latin '*moneo*' or '*monere*', which mean 'to remind'.

Column of Trajan

200 Built in 113 CE to commemorate Roman Emperor Trajan's victories against the Dacian tribes, the Column of Trajan is a gilded bronze column, 128 ft tall and 12 ft thick at the base, in Rome, Italy. It has a continuous frieze along the

length of the column, 218 ft long and 3 ft wide, with more than 2,500 human figures as well as hundreds of boats, horses, vehicles and military equipment. Trajan himself appears 58 times. Inside is a spiral staircase. The frieze winds around the column 23 times. In 1587, the top was crowned with a bronze figure of St. Peter.

201 **The first recorded Triumphal Arches were set up in the time of the Roman Republic.** They were set up to commemorate victories. Roman generals who triumphed in wars were called triumphators. Early in the 4th century CE, there were 36 such monuments in Rome.

202 **The Buland Darwaza ('Gate of Victory) was built by Mughal Emperor Akbar to commemorate his victory over Gujarat in 1601 CE.** The main gate to his Fatehpur Sikri palace near Agra, India, it is the highest gateway in the world. It is made of red sandstone, embellished by white and black marble, and is about 171 ft high.

203 **The Gateway of India in Mumbai was a magnificent structure to commemorate King George V and Queen Mary's visit to India in 1911, during British colonial rule.** Architect George Wittet designed it, overlooking the Arabian Sea, in yellow basalt stone. The 85 ft high, four-turreted gateway took 13 years to build.

India Gate

204 **Built by the British to commemorate 70,000 soldiers of the British Indian Army, who died during 1914–21 in the First World War, stands India Gate in Delhi, India.** Designed by

Edwin Lutyens and completed in 1931, it took ten years to build. There are 13,218 names – British and Indian – on the handsome 138 ft tall structure that stands on a base of red Bharatpur stone.

205 **Below India Gate's archway in Delhi is a black marble plinth with a reversed rifle capped by a war helmet surrounded by four eternal flames.** Built in 1972 after the 1971 Bangladesh War, it is the 'Amar Jawan Jyoti' ('Flame of the Immortal Soldier').

206 **Another National War Memorial, inaugurated in 2019, is in the vicinity of India Gate in Delhi.** It houses 21 busts of those awarded the Param Vir Chakra honour, and the names of those who lost their lives in peacekeeping missions and counter-insurgency operations. The site has an obelisk, an eternal flame and six bronze murals on battles fought by the Indian Armed Forces.

India's National War Memorial

207 **The Vietnam War Memorial in Washington, D.C., was designed by a young student, Maya Lin, and built in 1982.** Built a few steps below ground and etched on two 247-foot black granite walls, named the Veteran Memorial Walls, are 58,318 names of Americans dead or missing in action during the Vietnam War (1955–75). Standing proud next to it is a bronze statue, showing

three soldiers of Hispanic, African and European origins. It is the Servicemen Memorial. Next to that is the Women's Memorial Wall, where three nurses in uniform tend to a wounded soldier.

208 **A 70-second elevator ride (or 897 steps) takes you to the top of the Washington Monument, both the world's tallest stone structure in white and the world's tallest obelisk.** Standing tall at just over 554 ft 7 inches, and made of marble, granite, and bluestone gneiss, it honours George Washington, the first president of the USA. Started in 1848 and interrupted by the American Civil War, it was completed in 1884. A marble cornerstone 21 ft below ground has a zinc case filled with mementos.

209 **The Victoria Memorial is a large, 338 ft by 228 ft, marble building in Kolkata in West Bengal, India, built between 1906 and 1921 in the memory of Queen Victoria (1809–1901).** Designed in the Indo-Saracenic style, it has British, Mughal, Venetian, Egyptian and Islamic architectural elements. It rises to 184 ft and is now a museum.

210 **La Grande Arche, or Grande Arche de la Defense, in Paris, France, is almost a perfect cube – 360 ft in height, width and depth – but it's an arch.** It was built during president Francois Mitterand's tenure (in office 1981–95) to celebrate 'Humanity'. A massive square arch on 12 concrete pillars covered with 350,000 slabs of Carrara marble and 2,800 opaque glass panels, it has offices within and a road below.

211 **In Trafalgar Square in London, UK, there is a granite column standing on top of which is an 18 ft**

a tall sculpted statue of British Admiral Horatio Nelson. Designed by William Railton, the Nelson Column was built in 1843 to commemorate the British naval hero. The pedestal has four bronze relief panels, each 18 feet square, cast from captured French guns. They depict all his famous battles, including the Battle of Trafalgar in 1805, during which he was killed. The monument is 169 feet 3 inches tall. Four bronze lions on the base were added in 1867.

212 **On a massive 90 ft granite pedestal on Leninsky Avenue in Moscow, Russia, stands the 40 ft tall titanium statue of Soviet cosmonaut Yuri Gagarin.** It looks ready to take off, Superman-style. Erected in 1980, it commemorates the world's first human in space. Gagarin's 108-minute outing in outer space was in his Vostok spacecraft that completed one orbit of the Earth in 1961.

213 **The Gateway Arch on the river Mississippi in St. Louis, Missouri, was built as a monument to hail the westward expansion of the USA.** It is the world's tallest arch or steel parabola. Completed in 1965, it is covered in stainless steel and built as a 630 ft tall arch. An engineering marvel, it is earthquake-resistant. Designed to sway up to 18 inches, it can withstand winds of up to 240 km per hour.

214 **The Lincoln Memorial in Washington, D.C., USA, is a massive building shaped like a Greek temple, built to honour Abraham Lincoln, the 16th president of the USA, who led anti-slavery forces to victory.** His seated statue, within an 80 ft high and 188 ft long main chamber, can be seen through 36 huge columns, each signifying a state at the time of his death. Later, 12 more columns were built for new states. Designed by Henry Bacon and sculpted by Daniel

Lincoln Memorial

Chester French, the statue is 19 ft high and weighs 175 tonnes. The white Georgia marble for it had to be shipped in about 28 pieces. The memorial was built during 1918–22.

215 In Abraham Lincoln's second inaugural address, depicted on a wall of his memorial, an engraver, by mistake, carved a letter 'E' where he meant to carve an 'F', so the word 'FUTURE' became 'EUTURE'. This error was later corrected by filling in the base of the 'E'.

216 The **Mount Rushmore National Memorial** is a massive sculpture carved out of the rock sides of a mountain among the Black Hills of South Dakota, USA. Completed in 1941, the sculpture's 60 ft high granite faces of US presidents George Washington, Thomas Jefferson, Theodore Roosevelt and Abraham Lincoln look down upon you from a height. It records the first 130 years of the USA. In a chamber behind the carved faces is a vault with porcelain enamel panels with the American Declaration of Independence and the Constitution, the biographies of the

four presidents and Gutzon Borglum (who directed the construction of the memorial), and the history of the USA.

217 **Yad Vashem, a triangular structure with extraordinary cantilevered ends and skylights running across the top of a concrete building on the Mount of Remembrance in Jerusalem, is Israel's memorial to the Jewish victims of the Holocaust, perpetrated by the Nazis in Germany between 1941 and 1945.** Built in 1953 over 44.5 acres, it includes a circular 'Hall of Names' with brief write-ups on each victim over some two million pages and a nearly 33 ft high cone that displays photos and testimonies.

218 **The Marine Corps War Memorial in Virginia, USA, is based on a photo of the Battle of Iwo Jima by Pulitzer-Prize-winning iconic photographer Joe Rosenthal.** This was a major battle in which the US Marine Corps captured the island of Iwo Jima from the Imperial Japanese Army during the Second World War in 1945. The base, made of Swedish granite, bears inscriptions of the place and dates of every major battle involving the Marine Corps since 1775. It shows six 32 ft tall bronze marines standing on a granite base and planting a US flag into the ground.

219 **To celebrate his armies' victory over his enemies, Napoleon I had a triumphal arch, the Arc de Triomphe, built in 1806 in Paris, France.** It is 164 ft high and 148 ft wide, set in a circular plaza from which 12 grand avenues spread out in the shape of a star.

220 **The National September 11 Memorial and Museum in New York, USA, is dedicated to the victims of the 9/11 attacks.** It is a forest swamp of white oak trees with

221 **Standing on a hill 279 ft high in Russia's Volgograd (earlier Stalingrad) is the world's tallest statue of a woman.** 'The Motherland Calls' commemorates the bitterly fought Battle of Stalingrad during the Second World War, where the Soviet Union defended the city from German might. The figure of a woman stepping forward with a raised sword is said to be a mother calling on her sons and daughters to defend their motherland. Designed by sculptor Yevgeny Vuchetich and Nikolai Nikitin in 1967 and weighing 7,900 tonnes, it is a part of a monument ensemble called 'Heroes of the Battle of Stalingrad'. The concrete frame is supported by 99 metal cables.

two square reflecting pools in the centre marking where the twin towers of the World Trade Centre stood earlier. The pools are surrounded by panels with the names of people who died in the 1993 and 2001 terrorist attacks. It also has two of the largest man-made waterfalls in North America. A museum here contains artifacts, and personal stories.

222 **Though monuments are meant to be commemorative, any old beautiful building or site with ancient heritage value is now considered a monument. The UNESCO officially lists Italy with 53, China with 52, Spain with 46 and France with 43, while India has 29 such heritage sites.**

11

MOSQUES

Mosques serve as a place for prayer for Muslims, as well as for Ramazan vigils, funeral rituals, and for the collection and distribution of alms. Many mosques are also traditionally centres of early education and higher religious studies.

A mihrab

223 **No mosque is ever decorated with motifs of animals or human beings as Islam prohibits idol worship.** Geometric designs, leaves, flowers and words from the Quran written in calligraphy are generally used. There will always be a nook or a niche, called mihrab, in a wall facing Mecca, so that devotees can face that way.

224 **The Shah Cheragh mosque, meaning 'King of the Light', in Shiraz, Iran, was built around a grave that, it is said, emitted light.** In 900 CE, a curious traveller happened to stumble upon it, and found the body of an important Muslim religious leader in a shining armour. Though very ordinary looking from the outside, its ceiling and the walls are covered with millions and millions of

small mirror and glass pieces interspersed with an equal number of red, green, yellow and blue tiles, which reflect the sunlight to create a stunning effect. With sunlight coming in through large stained glass windows touching the floors and reflected by the mirrors, the whole effect is stunning.

225 **The Dome of the Rock on Temple Mount, part of a religious complex in the old city of Jerusalem, is of special significance to both Jews and Muslims.** Built by Umayyad Caliph Abd al-Malik in c. 692 over a 'rock', it is not actually a mosque but an Islamic shrine. The Jews believe this rock, now under a massive gold dome, was where their Prophet Abraham was preparing to kill his son Isaac because God asked him to, while the Muslims believe that it is from the same rock Prophet Muhammad ascended to heaven on a winged horse after a 'night journey' from Mecca. The stone bears a horse's imprint. A stairway leads to a natural cave below, known as the 'well of souls', where the souls of the dead are said to mingle with the waters of paradise on the way to eternity.

Dome of the Rock

226 Built by Emperor Justinian between 532 and 537 CE in what was then Constantinople, the Hagia Sophia in Istanbul, Turkey, was for the next 1,000 years a Christian

church. With the Muslim Ottomans coming to power in 1453, this famous church of the Middle Ages was turned into a mosque and so it has remained till in 1935 it became a museum. Instead of destroying the beautiful Christian mosaics Sultan Mehmet II plastered them over with striking Islamic motifs and designs, which have since been partially uncovered and restored.

227 **The largest, the oldest and the holiest of mosques in the world, the Great Mosque of Mecca or the Al-Masjid Al-Haram is in Mecca in Saudi Arabia.** Spread over 4,314,175 sq. ft, it is so large that during the 'Haj'– a pilgrimage that every Muslim must do once in a lifetime – it can accommodate four million worshippers at a time.

228 **Occupying pride of place in the centre of the Great Mosque of Mecca is the shrine of Kaaba.** To the Muslims it is the holiest place on earth. Roughly 50 ft high and about 35 by 40 ft at its base, it is made up of gray stone and marble. With three pillars and a few hanging silver and gold lamps, the shrine is usually kept covered in black brocade

229 **Built into the eastern wall of the Kaaba in the Great Mosque of Mecca is the Black Stone of Mecca.** This consists of some three large broken pieces, encircled by stones, and held together by a silver band. Every Haj pilgrim has to walk around the Kaaba seven times, as well as kiss and touch the Black Stone. They say that the stone was white to start with and that it turned black from taking on the sins of men.

230 **The Al Nabawi Mosque or the Prophet's Mosque in Medina, Saudi Arabia, is supposed to have been built by Prophet Muhammad himself.** It is also his final resting place. An unpainted cupola built above the tomb in the south-east corner of the mosque, dating back to 1279 CE, was painted green in 1837 and began to be known as the Green Dome.

231 **One of the most famous architectural landmarks in Africa is the Great Mosque of Djenne in Mali.** Built between 1200 and 1330 CE, it is the world's largest brick or adobe building and can hold 3,000 worshippers. Made of mud bricks and logs of wood which stick out, it needs constant attention as it is prone to cracks and erosion caused by weather changes. It has a main prayer wall or Qubla with three box-like minarets that jut out. The top of each minaret boasts of cone-shaped spires topped with ostrich eggs. It has arched doorways, rectangular pillars and innumerable vents to blow hot air out.

Great Mosque of Djenne

232 **One of the largest mosques in the world is the Sheikh Zayed Grand Mosque in Abu Dhabi, and it was built as recently as in 2007.** It took eleven years to build. As many as12,000 artisans worked day and night with stone, gold, crystals and semi-precious stones to produce a 30 acre (13,24,800 sq. ft) spread that boasts of 96 marble

pillars inlaid with mother-of-pearl and with Allah's 99 names on it and seven gold-gilded steel-and-brass Swarovski chandeliers made up of millions of crystals. With about 40 kg of 24-carat galvanized gold used in them, the largest is a 12-tonne chandelier that is 33 ft in diameter and 49 ft high. It also has an amazing 67,570 sq. ft hand-knotted woollen carpet, weighing around 35 tonnes, woven by 1,200 carpet workers for over two years.

233 **The stunning white Sheikh Zayed Grand Mosque in Abu Dhabi has 82 domes of various sizes.** With over 1,000 columns with reflective pools around them, the structure can hold more than 40,000 worshippers at a time. In a grand mix of Islamic styles, it also has four minarets at the corners. Since the Islamic calendar is the lunar one, a special lighting system that reflects the moonlight beams a soft bluish grey light from 22 light towers on the mosque that changes colour with the different phases of the moon. Named after the founder of the UAE, Sheikh Zayed bin Sultan Al Nahyan, it is also his final resting place.

234 **The Hagia Sophia in Istanbul, Turkey, has a large distinctive dome around, 102 ft in diameter and so heavy that the walls needed to be strengthened to hold it up.** It took 10,000 men five years, 10 months and four days to build the dome. From its construction in 537 to 1453, it served as a cathedral, and it was later converted into an Ottoman mosque from 29 May 1453 until 1931. Now it is a museum.

Hagia Sophia

235 **India has the largest number of active mosques in the world – about 300,000 of them. There are no mosques in Antarctica. Athens, the capital of Greece, is also the only capital in the world without a mosque.**

236 **The Cheraman Juma Mosque in Kodungalloor Kerala is the first mosque in India and the oldest mosque on the Indian subcontinent.** It was built in 629 CE by Malik Bin Dinar, an Arab Islamic preacher, on behalf of King Cheraman Perumal, who gave up his throne to become a Muslim and died while returning from Mecca. It has an ancient oil lamp that is always kept lit – since the day it was built more than 1,000 years ago.

237 **The Faisal Mosque in Islamabad, Pakistan, is designed to look like a Bedouin desert tent. Built in 1976 and named after King Faisal of Saudi Arabia, who put up most of the money, this building has four 260 ft stunning minarets and no dome.**

238 **The Quba Mosque in Medina, Saudi Arabia, is considered to be the first mosque ever built.** Originally an open-air mosque, believed to have been built in 622 CE, it still retains some original features despite renovations. It has seven main entrances and 12 smaller ones, four minarets, 56 domes, a library and a shopping complex too.

239 **A mosque honoured by both Christians and Muslims is the Great Mosque or Umayyad Mosque of Damascus.** Built by Umayyad Caliph al-Walid in the early 8th century, it was first a temple dedicated to the Greek God Jupiter and then a Christian basilica dedicated to John the Baptist, a prophet revered both by Christians and Muslims, before it became a mosque. Supported by Greek Corinthian columns, it has John the Baptist's head among its relics.

240 **The Crystal Mosque in Malaysia is not big but is one of the most beautiful mosques built. Built in 2008, in steel, glass and crystal, it blends Chinese and Islamic architectural styles. When lit, it glows from inside causing the glass domes to gleam.**

Crystal Mosque

241 **Built by Sultan Bayezid I between 1396 and 1399, the Bursa Mosque in Turkey has 20 domes and two minarets.** But that is not all! It is covered in exquisite Islamic calligraphy found nowhere else in the world. As many as 192 wall inscriptions by 41 famous Ottoman calligraphers in 13 different writing styles grace the inside. The entire solar system, with the sun and all its planets correctly aligned, etched in wood, is another unique feature.

242 **Delhi's Jama Masjid meaning 'Friday mosque' is the largest mosque in India and the tenth largest in the world.** Made of red sandstone and marble, it was built by Mughal Emperor Shah Jahan between 1644 and 1656. Two minarets 130 feet tall and three large marble domes grace the building. There are 260

Delhi's Jama Masjid

columns in the huge main hall. It is about 500 m away from another architectural marvel – the Red Fort.

243 **The Moscow Cathedral Mosque Russia is the largest mosque in Europe.** Built first in 1904, it has six storeys and turquoise and golden cupolas. Around 12 tonnes of gold cover its 151 ft dome and its minarets, one of which has a crescent on top, are decorated with Turkish mosaics and ornamentation.

244 **The minaret of the Hassan II Mosque in Casablanca, Morocco, is the tallest minaret in the world.** Built in 1993, the 689 ft high structure has a laser on top – extending about 32 km – pointing across the sea towards Mecca.

Hassan II Mosque

12

MUSEUMS

Museums are, more often than not, architecturally beautiful buildings that house ancient cultural artefacts. These objects of art throw up our past and enrich our knowledge data bank, while the buildings themselves become an expression of art or the theme of the museum.

245 **An amazing glass and metal pyramid surrounded by three smaller ones in the main forecourt stand at odds with the Louvre in Paris, France, an 18th century palace for French Kings.** Converted into a museum with some of the world's must-see best paintings and artefacts, the old Louvre palace, opened in 1793, couldn't handle the number of visitors who came to see it. So in 1989, architect I.M. Pei, designed a cluster of modern pyramids here, four above ground plus one suspended upside down, visible only underground. He created a lobby under the pyramids, as the main entrance to the Louvre Museum. At its base, the main pyramid is 116 ft wide and 70 ft high, with 673 glass panes, 95 tonnes of steel and 105 tonnes of aluminium supporting it. Its specifications are almost the same as those of the Great

Louvre Museum

Pyramid of Giza built in the 3rd century, which – at almost 50 storeys high – was the tallest building in the world for over 3,800 years.

246 **With an area size of 782,910 sq. ft, the Louvre Museum is today the largest and the most visited museum in the world.** More than 7.4 million people visit it every year. It displays more than 380,000 objects, which include sculptures, paintings, drawings, objets d'art and archaeological finds.

247 **A 'living roof' with trays of about 1.7 million plants covers the California Academy of Sciences in San Francisco, naturally 'alive' museum.** It is the largest science and natural history museum in the world, with an aquarium and a planetarium too. A beautiful habitat for birds, butterflies and other local wildlife, it has a collection of 260,000 species.

248 **There are more than 55,000 museums in the world. The world's first and oldest university art museum, the Ashmolean Museum in Oxford, UK, opened in 1683. It was Britain's first public museum as well.**

249 **An art museum that looks like nothing on earth is the Kunsthaus Graz Art Museum in Graz Austria.** Designed by architects Peter Cook and Colin Fournier, it is a bulbous building with skylight shafts jutting out from the top like a metallic giant heart or an outlandish creature. With nearly 1,000 embedded fluorescent rings programmed to create patterns, the building looks spectacularly alien at night.

250 Built from 3,400 individual wooden elements and 3,000 load-bearing connection nodes, Metropol

Parasol in Seville, Spain, is an archaeological museum in the shape of six parasols that look like giant mushrooms. Designed by architect Jurgen Mayer, it is the largest wooden structure in the world with wood pieces, 54 ft long and ranging in thickness from 0.22 to 1 ft, it includes an antiquarium, where Roman and Moorish remains discovered on site are displayed. It is said to be inspired by the ancient vaults of the Seville cathedral and the Ficus trees growing around it.

Metropol Parasol

251 **The Solomon R. Guggenheim Museum of Art in New York, built in 1959, is the extraordinary shape of a spiral nautilus shell.** A reported 7,000 cubic ft of concrete and 700 tonnes of steel were used for just its structure and shell. Developed from 700 sketches and six sets of working drawings by architect Frank Lloyd Wright, this conch-shaped building was a world trendsetter in architecture.

252 **The Virasat-e-Khalsa, a Sikh heritage museum designed by Moshe Safdie Architects, in Anandpur Sahib, Punjab, is holds the record for the highest daily footfall in a museum in India.** Commissioned by the Government of Punjab in 1999 to commemorate the tercentenary year of the Birth of the Khalsa, the complex has a series of cylindrical, square and triangular tower-like shafts, covered in hand-chiselled Gwalior sandstone and reflecting the fort architecture of Punjab and Northern India. The 100-acre

site houses columnar arcades, traditional sacred courtyards and ceremonial pools, terraces and hanging gardens.

253 **Two huge sculptures – a 39 ft high 'Puppy' made of flowers and a 33 ft tall 'Spider' of bronze, steel and marble – welcome you to the famous Guggenheim Museum of Art in Bilbao, Spain.** Spread over 260,000 sq. ft, it is an impressive structure made of titanium, limestone and glass. As many as 33,000 very thin titanium sheets in curved, wave-like shapes interspersed with covered stone and large glass walls form the outside. Built around a central hall that is 164 ft high, it is topped by a metal dome. Curved bridges, glass elevators and tower-like staircases connect the 19 galleries spread over three floors. It is said that architect Frank Gehry tested 29 types of metals before settling for titanium.

Spain's Guggenheim Museum of Art

254 The **Guggenheim Abu Dhabi Museum,** spread over 450,000 sq. ft, promises to be a spectacular building on the Arabian waterfront. Frank Gehry has used the concept of the historic wind-towers of the UAE for ventilation and shade here, besides fusing Islamic and Middle Eastern styles. An enormous cone in the centre and eleven more, housing galleries, surrounding it will act as wind-towers.

255 **The Louvre Museum in Abu Dhabi and the Abu Dhabi government paid the French government half a billion dollars to use the name 'Louvre'.**

The Louvre Abu Dhabi

256 **Designed by Jean Nouvel, the Louvre Abu Dhabi, which opened in 2017, looks like it has a floating dome, due to its hidden pillars.** The silver-latticed dome is layered with almost 8,000 small patterned slits through which the light filters in, creating a rain-like effect. The thatched palm-leaf look gives the roof an Arabian touch. It has 23 permanent galleries all styled like medinas and low-lying Arab settlements.

257 **The Singapore's ArtScience Museum on Marina Bay often referred to as 'The Welcoming Hand of Singapore'.** And with good reason. Designed by architect Moshe Safdie, it is in the shape of half a lotus, seemingly anchored by a round base with ten fingerlike extensions. Each finger is an exhibiting gallery and has skylights at the 'fingertips'. With 21 gallery spaces spread over 50,000 sq. ft, it is the world's first ArtScience Museum. And guess how it gets its water? Rainwater harvested and channelled to flow through the centre via the bowl-shaped roof into a reflecting pond at the bottom is recycled for use in the restrooms.

258 **The Milwaukee Art Museum looks like a modern cathedral with its flying buttresses, pointed arches, ribbed vaults and a central nave topped by a 90 ft high glass roof.** The main hall, resembling the front of a ship, has floor-to-ceiling windows that overlook Lake Michigan. It houses more than 30,000 artworks in its 142,050 sq. ft structure, completed in 2001.

259 **Designed by Spanish architect Santiago Calatrava, the Milwaukee Art Museum's Quadracci Pavilion has an enormous movable sunscreen roof.** Called the 'Burke Brise Soleil', it weighs 90 tonnes and is made up of 72 steel fins ranging in length from 26 to 105 ft, that look like wings. It takes 3.5 minutes for these 'wings' to open or close. Sensors on the fins continually monitor wind speed and direction, so when winds exceed 37 kmph for more than three seconds, the wings close automatically.

260 **Resembling a ship in full sail, the Louis Vuitton Foundation of Contemporary Art in Paris, France, built on the edge of a water garden is a modern architectural marvel in glass.** Curved glass panels attached to a steel frame form the covering. It has white blocks known as 'the icebergs', which are clad in 19,000 panels of white fibre-reinforced concrete, and surrounded by 12 large glass sails, supported by wooden beams and made of 3,600 carved glass panels. The glass roof allows the building to collect and reuse rainwater. The museum has 11 exhibition galleries. Frank Gehry used digital software to create his design, ending up with close to 190,000 digital files.

261 **In a corner of Shanghai is the Liuli China Museum, the world's first Liuli art museum.** Liuli is the ancient Chinese name of the coloured glass crystal unique to China. The 10,764 sq. ft museum's exterior wall is made up of 12,000 individually made glass bricks, each 11.8 x 11.8 x 11.68 inches, and weighing 10 kg. Sculpted from delicate metal wires and made up of 5,025 handmade petals weighing 1.5 tonnes, the peony flower on the facade blooms at night, emitting a fiery red light. Founded by Liuli artists Loretta H.

Yang and Chang Yi, this museum has some of China's oldest glass artefacts as also glass art from the rest of the world.

262 **The world's largest research and museum complex in the world is the famous Smithsonian in Washington, D.C., USA.** Designed as a castle by James Renwick Jr., a famous architect, it was constructed from red sandstone. It has 19 museums and galleries plus the National Zoological Park. It is estimated that if you spend one minute at each exhibit here, it would take you more than 250 years to see them all. Built in 1855, the building was designed by James Renwick Junior and built in red sandstone in Gothic and Romanesque styles.

263 **The Metropolitan Museum of Art in New York, USA, known popularly as the 'Met', is the fourth largest museum in the world.** Opened in February 1872, it has about 5,000 musical instruments, among two million other exhibits, including the world's oldest piano dated to 1720. It has blocks of uncarved rough stones on top of its columns, which is at odds with the rest of the building. These were meant to be 31 pieces of sculptures for the entrance but a lack of funds left them unfinished. Now it is an accepted part of its facade.

264 **The second largest art museum in the world after the Louvre is the famous State Hermitage Museum in**

Hermitage Museum

St. Petersburg, Russia. Built and rebuilt during 1754–62 on the banks of the river Neva, it was once known as the 'Winter Palace' and home to the Russian royalty till 1917. This architecturally stunning palace in white, green and gold now has 2,000 rooms of exhibits, with over three and a half million cultural pieces and the world's largest selection of paintings.

265 **Near the 'singing sands' of Kotogahama Beach is the six-pyramid Nimes Sand Museum in Japan, designed by Shin Takamatsu and opened in 1991.** The tallest pyramid stands 69 ft high with a 56 ft base and houses the world's largest hourglass, which measures a whole year! Designed in glass and steel, the other five pyramids contain sand clocks from across the world and art exhibits made from Nima's sand dunes. When walked upon, the sand dunes squeak lyrically. 'Singing sands' are found in only a few dozen locations around the world and this is one.

266 **The world's most unusual museum, possibly, is the Shit Museum or the Museo Della Merde founded in Lombardy, Italy, in 2015 by agriculturalist Gianantonio Locatelli.** His herd of 3,500 cows produces 50,000 litres of milk a day, used to make cheese. The cows also produce around 150,000 kg of dung. So Locatelli decided to convert the dung into manure for his farm. And also started a museum with many faeces-related artefacts including lumps of fossilized dinosaur faeces, jars of faeces, and artworks inspired by human waste.

13

NATURE-INSPIRED BUILDINGS

From the earliest times, humans have been inspired by Nature when it comes to design and architecture. Now biomimicry has helped to visualize and construct some spectacular buildings round the world.

267 **Transparent House in Tokyo, Japan, has hardly any walls.** Large glass windows let in plenty of daylight and the idea is to live as free and open as on a tree. Its white steel-frame structure itself has no resemblance to a tree, but the design appears to imitate a tree with different levels of open living space in a three-storeyed building. 'House NA', as it is known, is architect Sou Fukimoto idea of a modern tree house. Unfortunately, you will have no privacy or a place to hide.

268 **The Lotus Temple in Delhi has been inspired by what else but the lotus flower.** Twenty-seven free-standing marble-clad petals in clusters of three form nine sides of this

Lotus Temple

temple of the Baha'i faith. Designed by Iranian architect Fariborz Sahba, the building has nine entrances that open into a huge central hall meant for prayer. Sitting on 26 acres of land amidst lovely landscaped gardens, it also has nine ponds. Nine, as you may have guessed, is an auspicious number in the Baha'i faith.

269 **Another tree-inspired building is the Taipei 101 in Taiwan, once the tallest skyscraper in the world.** Taking inspiration from the local bamboo plant, it spreads skywards exactly like a bamboo stalk and was designed by C.Y. Lee & Partners. It is an eco-friendly building too.

270 **Made from a steel space frame clad with ETFE-fluorine based plastic, the Beijing National Aquatics Center looks like an enormous water cube with bubbles.** Built for the 2008 Summer Olympics it is naturally well lit and can fit in from 7,000 to 17,000 people.

Beijing National Aquatics Center

271 **Algae House in Hamburg, Germany, has the world's first 'bioreactor facade' or bio-powered building.** It is a five-storey building with two differently designed facade types. The green tower is largely transparent and on the facade that faces the sun, micro algae – tiny

plants, no bigger than bacteria – are produced, allowing the building to supply its own energy. They control and filter the amount of light the building needs and the shade required. When enough algae have grown, they are harvested to make biogas to run the whole building.

272 **Inspired by how the 'cactus' works in the desert the Office of the Minister of Municipal Affairs and Agriculture in Doha, Qatar, boasts of a towering cactus-shaped building.** This amazing piece of desert technology has sunshade panels on its windows that open and shut depending on the sun's strength, just like the cactus. Cacti perform transpiration at night instead of the day to retain water, so the building also 'biomimics' the same action. It also has a botanic dome with a botanic garden at its base and is energy efficient.

273 **The 'Palm Islands' in Dubai, UAE, are three artificial man-made islands in the shape of palm trees.**

Palm Islands, as seen from above

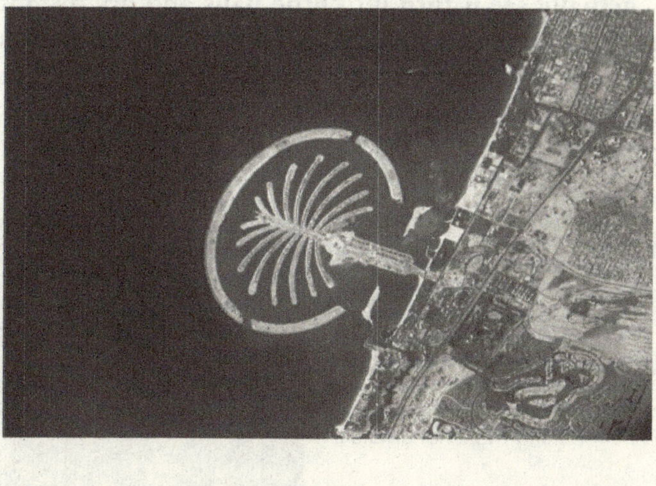

Beautifully landscaped and strikingly well laid out, they have both offices and residential apartments. One of them – the recently completed Palm Jumeirah – is visually stunning with a crescent on top. It is similar to a palm frond that grows wild in the desert.

274 **The National Taichung Theater in Taiwan takes its inspiration from flowing water.** Spread over 620,920 sq. ft, it resembles a coral reef with curved irregular entrances and openings. The entire eight-storey theatre has walls that appear to flow into the ceiling with no clear boundaries or lines. Toyo Ito, the designer–architect, has said that he drew inspiration from the formation of rocks, caves and the impermanence of water.

275 **The nature-inspired Ceracasa is a ceramic tile that cleans the air by breaking down pollutants. Treated with a titanium dioxide glaze, it mimics the design of the leaves of trees with the same micro-textures that help to purify the air.**

276 **If you pour water on a 'Silgranit' surface, you will actually see it turn into little balls and dry instantly.** Blanco Silgranit is a material used for kitchen sinks as it is hydrophobic (that means it repels water). It imitates the action of butterflies drying their wings without leaving any water stains. So the next best thing for kitchens is already here!

277 A giant bird's nest made out of 110,000 tonnes of steel is what the Beijing National Stadium in China

Beijing National Stadium

looks likes. Built for the 2008 Olympics, it is also the world's largest steel structure, with 26 km of unwrapped steel in a wire mesh pattern. Its circular shape is meant to represent heaven, but a bird's nest is what it is popularly called!

278 **There is a building in India, inspired by the 'Hyperion', the tallest tree in the world found in California.** 'Hyperions' in Jaypee Sports City in Delhi is made of six garden towers, each 36-storey high, with residential and office spaces. A cluster of buildings made of wood, it also has carrots, tomatoes, spinach, saffron and coriander grown – in clay balls – on each apartment's balcony. A network of suspended walkways connects the towers. Developed by Vincent Callebaut Architectures, it features edible vegetation that can be grown up and around wooden and timber towers.

279 **The Lotus Exhibition Center city of Wujin China is underground, with a lake on top!** In the centre of the lake are three sculptural and almost translucent lotuses displaying the three stages of the bloom's life cycle. The inside of the central flower is a sand and stainless steel hexagon mosaic in various shades of white, which ends at the top with a 26 ft high chandelier.

280 The **Cube Houses of Rotterdam in the Netherlands are architecturally astounding.** All the walls are slanted, they are asymmetrical and represent an abstract

Cube Houses

forest, with each triangular roof representing a treetop. Designed by Dutch architect Piet Blom, it is a residential complex where all the homes are literally cubes, tilted at 45 degree angles. The entrance to each of the three-level house lies inside the concrete 'trunk' that has a staircase. Amazingly, it also forms a pedestrian bridge across one of Rotterdam's main thoroughfares.

281 **At the entrance of the main market in Vallero Square in Jerusalem, Israel, are four giant inflatable red poppies, called 'Warde'.** Though technically not a building, they are 30 ft high and 30 ft wide, and they open and close depending on how close the shoppers are. When people walk by, the flowers inflate and open up. They stay open as long as any person remains near it. When they walk away, they close up. Since it's near a tram station, all four flowers inflate when trams approach. At night the lights in the centre of the poppies light up the place.

282 **The Redwood Treehouse in Warkworth, north of Auckland in New Zealand, draws inspiration from cocoons.** This 32.8ft high, pod-shaped structure on a redwood tree is a 50-seater restaurant, reached by an elevated wooden walkway.

283 **The Gherkin in London, UK, is a 590 ft tower that has 41 floors and an air ventilation system similar to sea sponges and anemones.** Completed in 2004, it is considered one of the best examples of environmentally friendly modern buildings. There are gaps within it that form shafts, which create a giant double-glazing effect. With air sandwiched between two layers of glazing, it naturally insulates the office space inside, just like in sponges.

284 **The Sagrada Familia Cathedral in Barcelona, Spain, is still in the process of being constructed even 100 years after the death of its architect and designer Antoni Gaudi.** Designed like a tree with awesome twisting branchlike columns supporting the roof, and skylights of green and gold to filter in the sunlight through large coloured windows, its entire interior has been inspired by a forest. It also has a turtle at the base and a tortoise to represent sea and land. The mosaic on the roof acts like a lighthouse in the moonlight. Started in 1883, this spectacular church is planned to be completed by 2026. Gaudi died in 1926.

285 **The clam-shell inspired Aldar Headquarters Building in Abu Dhabi, UAE, is 20–100 storeys high and was voted the Best Futuristic Design of 2008.** Steel grids were used to maintain its shape. Its curved glass skin – most difficult to build – became part of the external diamond-shaped steel structure called a diagrid, which gives the building its striking shape.

286 **The headquarters of the Wison Company in Shanghai, China, is built around a central atrium, shaped like a blossoming flower.** Built according to Feng Shui principles, its five wings, with seven to ten storeys of office space, have facades of glass panels, while the main building is made of printed white glass.

287 **The Widnes Waterfront Future Flower is a wind-powered, nearly 46 ft high metallic flower beside the river Mersey in the UK.** It is made of triangles and pentagons of steel, and has 120 galvanized steel petals fixed to a central stalk, which has branches that can hold 60 watts of LED lights aimed at different clusters of petals. The lights are powered by mini turbines attached to the stem. The speed of the wind triggers off the lights.

288 **Sibelius Hall by the beautiful Lake Vesijarvi in Lahti, Finland, is the biggest public wooden building constructed in Finland in over a hundred years.** More than 70 per cent of Finland is forest and Finnish people look to their trees for peace, calm and quiet. Inspired entirely by the relaxing quality of forests, architects Kimmo Lintula and Hannu Tikka designed this amazing concert hall in 2000, entirely out of glulam.

289 **'Glulam' is short for glue-laminated timber. It has many layers of solid wood lumber bonded together with an adhesive to form a panel.**

14

OPERA HOUSES, THEATRES AND CONCERT HALLS

Most opera houses or theatres or concert halls are housed in beautiful buildings with velvet curtains, a marvellous stage and brilliant acoustics. They host operas, ballets, plays, musicals and other outstanding art performances.

290 The Odeon of Herodes Atticus in Athens, Greece, is one of the oldest concert halls still in use. A steep-sloped stone theatre structure, it was built by magnate Herodotus Atticus in 161 CE, in memory of his wife, and renovated in 1950.

Ruins of the Odeon of Herodes Atticus

291 **Built between 1744 and 1748 and designed by Giuseppe Galli Bibiena, the Margravial Opera House in Bayreuth, Germany, is the only surviving royal court opera house in the grand Baroque style of architecture.** With gilted stucco, interiors studded with red, green and gold gems, and crystal chandeliers that twinkle and sparkle, this 520-seat box theatre is a UNESCO heritage site.

292 **With cascading plants, painted plant murals, trellises and lamp posts dressed in real dry leaves, the Winter Garden Theater in Toronto, Canada, has lantern lights inspired by Nature and columns that are trees.** The stage too is like the outdoor night with an inky sky, clouds and a bright moon. The roof garden theatre was part of the seven-storeyed Elgin cinema-theatre complex popular in the 1920s. It closed down for a while, but was renovated in 1980, when they worked in 5,000 beech branches back into the garden ceiling of the world's only double-decker theatre.

293 **A replica of the original Globe Theatre – yes, of Shakespeare's company – was built in 1997 very close to where the original one was in London, UK.** While maintaining the look of the old one (built in 1599 and destroyed in a fire in 1613), the 857-seater Shakespeare's Globe has modern features such as roof sprinklers and a concrete theatre pit. It has a unique roof, the only thatched one allowed in London since the Great Fire of 1666.

Shakespeare's Globe

294 **The National Noh Theatre in Tokyo, Japan, was constructed in 1983 from 400-year-old cypress trees! Its seats have a personal subtitling system that can be changed from Japanese to English with the press of a button.**

295 The **Palais Garnier or the 'Paris Opera'** in Paris, France, is known after its architect Charles Garnier. Built from 1861 to 1875, it features two amazing bronze statues

holding torches on the facade. Chandeliers and mirrors are spread all over its rooms with one enormous eight-tonne one with 340 lights hanging in the centre. A huge salamander – a lizard-like creature – lies halfway up the balustrade on its stunning 98 ft high, multicoloured marble grand staircase. They say salamanders escape fires due to their moist skin; this opera house had its share of fires over the years, so a stone salamander was included as a superstition.

296 **Made up of more than 45 different types of marble from across the world, the Paris Opera House, once the world's largest theatre, took 15 years to build.** Its 177 ft long, 42.5 ft wide and 59 ft high foyer is almost blinding in its gold decoration. A striking bust of the architect Charles Garnier sits at the entrance. The horseshoe-shaped auditorium seats 2,000 people. The ceiling has scenes from operas of 14 famous composers, added on almost 90 years later, in 1964.

297 **The Paris Opera House became the inspiration for the famous novel and musical the 'Phantom of the Opera'.** This happened after a chandelier's counterweight broke loose and crashed down, killing a seated theatregoer and injuring a few others. There is a lake and some cellars below

Paris Opera House

the theatre where the phantom was supposed to have lived and Box Number 5 is where he sat.

298 **The Tokyo Opera City Concert Hall looks like any other conventional hall, but glance up, and you will be stunned to see the ceiling merge into an enormous pyramid with wooden grooves and walls almost sloping at the apex, Egyptian style. Another surprise – it is in a skyscraper! One of the tallest buildings in Tokyo, it can seat 1,800 people.**

299 **Birds – 340,000 of them – in light grey to black carved in seven different shapes and four shades are ready for a grand take-off on the stunning exterior of the Philharmonie de Paris, France.** With a rooftop that is 121 ft high and its wavy-curving wood-finish basket-weave panels, its every wall and corner is carefully shaped to enhance sound reflections. Designed by architect Jean Nouvel and built in 2015, it can accommodate 2,400 people among balconies that appear to float around the central stage.

300 **The Teatro Amazonas or the Amazon Theater is right in the middle of the Amazonian rainforests in Brazil!** It was designed by Italian architect Celestial Sacardim, who shipped roof tiles and furniture from France, Italian marble for its stairs and columns and Glasgow steel for its walls. Located in Manaus, its outer dome is decorated with 36,000 ceramic tiles painted in the colors of the Brazilian national flag. After the first performance in 1897, it didn't function until it was reopened in the 1990s.

301 **With its roof that looks like white, shell-shaped sails, the Sydney Opera House has been sitting grandly overlooking the Sydney Harbor since 1973.** It took 14 years to build. Designed by Jorn Utzon from Denmark

Sydney Opera House

who won the contest for its design from among 233 international designs, it is today considered the greatest architectural work of the 20th century. Its roofs have a total of 1,056,006 tiles.

302 **Believe it or not, seven A380s could sit wing-to-wing on the Sydney Opera House site.** Spread over 4.4 acres, it is 1,83,600 ft long and 394 ft wide. As many as 588 concrete piers sunk 82 ft below sea level support it, while more than a million Swedish roof tiles cover it. It can seat 5,700 people. Pipes – 35 km long – carry sea water to power the hot and cold air-conditioning in the building.

303 **The National Centre for the Performing Arts in Beijing, China, is in the shape of a gigantic titanium-and-glass egg atop a man-made lake.** Seating more than 5,400 people across its three halls, it is connected to land by a 196.8 ft long transparent underpass. This curved building, covered in gilt mesh and designed by French architect Paul Andreu, located next to the ancient Forbidden City in Beijing, is an iconic modern structure.

The titanium shell in the shape of a super ellipsoid, 151 ft high, is divided in two.

304 **The Harpa Concert Hall in Reykjavík, Iceland, is a multicoloured glass-clad steel structure that brightens up the dark Icelandic environment like a rainbow-coloured iceberg.** Designed by artist Olafur Eliasson, this 141 ft building has 714 irregularly shaped glass hexagon panels with built-in LEDs that reflect the light of the Northern Lights as well. So night or day, summer or winter, the effect of light on the building is simply amazing.

Harpa Concert Hall

305 **Everyone's heard of Broadway in New York, USA, but what's Off-Broadway? Broadway theatre buildings have 500 seats, Off-Broadway have 100-499 seats and Off-Off-Broadway have less than hundred.**

306 **A striking statue of Apollo driving a four-horse chariot above its eight-column portico is what catches**

307 **The Minack Theatre in Cornwall, UK, is a world famous open-air theatre with a war story behind it.** After the First World War (1914–18) a young girl called Rowena Cade moved to Cornwall with her mother, and built a home at Minack Point. When a local village group needed a place to stage their Shakespearean play, *The Tempest*, Miss Cade offered her garden overlooking the sea. She and her gardener made a terrace for the stage and enough rough seating for an audience. The play with the sea as a backdrop was a grand hit and a cliff-side auditorium was born. The theatre now looks carved into the 2,000-year-old granite cliff overlooking the Porthcurno Bay and is set amid lovely gardens. Some 80,000 people come here yearly for a show, and more than 100,000 just to look around the place.

the eye as you drive up to the Bolshoi Theatre in Moscow, Russia. This 'Quadriga of Apollo' symbolizes the eternal movement of art and life. The word Bolshoi means 'large or grand'. With an elegant square and a classical fountain in its forecourt the Bolshoi was first founded in 1776, presenting operas and ballets from Bolshoi opera and ballet companies. Destroyed a few times since its inception, the theatre took its present form in 1825. It is decorated in red and gold tapestries, murals on the ceilings and 42 crystal chandeliers, including one two-tonne one with 24,000 pendants.

308 **Every year, as a tradition, the Moscow authorities plant two varieties of tulips in front of the theatre, which seats 2,153 people.** Its heavy curtain of natural silk and metallic thread, with a very thin layer of gold covering, measures 5,382 sq. ft and weighs more than a tonne.

309 The very modern **Metropolitan Opera House, New York,** built in 1966 in the Lincoln Center, has a huge 23-karat gold leaf that covers the entire ceiling, made of more than 4,000 gold squares. Two large murals by the famous painter Marc Chagall, 'The Triumph of Music' and 'The Sources of Music', with clusters of 21 sparkling Swarovski crystal chandeliers, adorn the lobby. The chandeliers were a gift from the Austrian government to thank America for its aid in the years following the First World War.

Dusseldorfer Schauspielhaus theatre

310 **The Dusseldorfer Schauspielhaus theatre in Dusseldorf, Germany, which replaced the old one presented**

in 1818 by King Friedrich Wilhelm II of Prussia to the city residents as a gift, was designed by architect Bernhard Pfau to look like an undulating theatre curtain.

311 **The Symphony Hall in Boston, USA, owes a lot to a physics professor from Harvard University.** In the late 19th century, Wallace Clement Sabine was the first to conduct scientific measurements to understand how sound behaves in a room and the concert hall, completed in 1900, incorporated his findings.

312 **You can get to walk all over the roof of the Oslo Opera House in Norway.** At the edge of the waterfront, covered in Italian marble and white granite, overlooking the Oslo Fjord, it appears to emerge from the water like a giant angular iceberg with its crystal blue glass windows. In contrast, inside it has curvy wooden walls and warm yellow lighting. Spread over 414,000 sq. ft. and is the largest building in Norway. Built in 2008, it seats about 1,900 people across its three stages. Its horizontal sloping 'carpet'-like surface or ramp makes for easy accessibility and a unique look.

Oslo Opera House

313 **Have you ever wondered why the insides of a theatre or concert hall traditionally had so much wood?** Sweeping, sloping wooden walls, curving wave like wooden ceilings, balconies with wood finish, wood backrests for seats and wooden floorboards... Wood is a good conductor of sound and makes for good acoustics.

314 The Berlin Philharmonie, which opened in 1963, is known for its architect Hans Scharoun's new concept of vineyard terracing for top acoustics! By dividing the audience areas into blocks, the in-between walls were used to reflect more sound to the audience.

315 **The fancy sweeping and curvy panels hanging from the ceiling in the new Philharmonie de Paris have a function!** They are designed to enhance sound reflections into the audience. The building also houses a museum that follows the history of music from the 17th century to the present through the instruments used.

316 **The Pula Arena is a very special place in Croatia.** It is the only surviving Roman amphitheatre to have four side towers and all three sides fully preserved. It was constructed between 27 BCE and 68 CE and is now used for concerts.

317 **Teatru Manoel in Valetta, Malta, is one of Europe's oldest functioning theatres! Built in 1731, it survived both World Wars, despite serving as a bomb shelter during the second one!**

15

PALACES

What 'houses' are to us, 'palaces' are to kings and queens. They are large and impressive buildings that are the official residence of a ruler. Here are just a few grand and historically important imperial residences.

318 ***'Palatium'* in Latin means a palace, especially the palace of an ancient Roman emperor.** Even if we were to build ourselves a grand residence, it does not become a 'palace', however 'palatial' it might be. It is considered a palace when the person residing in it is the country's ruler and occupies it officially. Sometimes residences of Popes, archbishops and other spiritual leaders are also called 'palaces'.

319 **A palace is different from a castle.** A castle is a fortified palace. It will normally have thick walls, lookouts, turrets and towers with a moat or a large channel of water running around it. Medieval in character, it has all the safeguards for protection against the enemy. A palace, on the other hand, is more an enormously large and lavishly decorated residence with none of the protective architectural safeguards.

320 **Due to periodic renovations, most palaces have a combination of architectural styles.** The Schonbrunn Palace, for instance, the home of the Hapsburg Royals

Schonbrunn Palace

in Vienna, Austria, was built between 1696 and 1712 in the Baroque style. Rooms renovated later in the 19th century boast of the Rococo Revival style (flowers and exotic motifs), including the magnificent white and gold 'Mirrors Room' with its numerous crystal mirrors. One of the most impressive palaces in Europe, it sits high on a hill and has 1,441 exquisitely furnished rooms.

321 **There is a zoo within the palace estate of Schonbrunn Palace.** Founded in 1752, it is the oldest known zoo in the world and is home to more than 750 kinds of animals as different as giant pandas, orangutans, Siberian tigers, African elephants, cheetahs, koalas, penguin and Arctic wolves.

322 **The Schonbrunn Palace also has a maze,** built between 1698 and 1740. It was once a royal strolling four-way path with a raised central pavilion overlooking it. Redone in 1998, the 18,640 sq. ft labyrinth is now a fun place for visitors. It actually has three mazes that include a 'chiming' climbing pole with a bell on top, a giant kaleidoscope,

zodiac signs, mathematical riddles and numbered stepping stones that tell you how many steps you're allowed to take. And finally, you can also watch everybody else who is lost in it from a special platform.

323 **One of the oldest and the largest surviving palaces in the world is the Topkapi Palace in Istanbul, Turkey, built by Sultan Mehmet between 1466 and 1478. It was home to the Ottoman Sultans for 400 years till 1853 and turned into a museum in 1924.**

Topkapi Palace

324 **Many of the world's past treasures are still housed in the Topkapi Palace in Istanbul, Turkey.** Among them is the famous emerald-studded Topkapi dagger in its diamond-and-enamel-studded sheath. The film *Topkapi* was based on this dagger that the then Sultan of the Ottoman Empire had made for Nadir Shah of Persia in 1747. But the Shah was assassinated before it reached him. The 'Pavilion of the Holy Mantle' holds relics of Prophet Muhammad. It also has some 10,000 porcelain pieces including a 14th-century bowl that changes colour when it comes in contact with poisonous food.

325 **Many palaces continue to be imperial residences even today.** For instance, the Buckingham Palace in London, UK, which was built in 1703, became a royal home in 1837 when Queen Victoria moved in. Her great-great-granddaughter Queen Elizabeth II currently lives there. This palace has 775 rooms, spread over 830,000 sq. ft, including 19 state rooms, 52 royal and guest bedrooms, 188 staff bedrooms, 92 offices, 78 bathrooms and 350 clocks. It has its own chapel, post office, swimming pool, staff cafeteria, doctor's surgery, cinema and ATM.

326 **The Lake Palace (or Taj Lake Palace) was built between 1743 and 1746 under the direction of the Maharana Jagat Singh II of Udaipur in Rajasthan, India, as a winter palace.** Its features include fountains, gardens and pillared terraces. It was initially called Jagniwas or Jan Niwas after its founder. Located on an island on Lake Pichola, and now a hotel, its foundation spans four acres. Guests are transported to the hotel by a speedboat from a jetty. Its walls, made of black and white marble, were inlaid with semi-precious stones and had ornamented niches. Gardens, fountains, pillared terraces and columns line its courtyards.

327 **Umaid Bhawan Palace in Jodhpur in Rajasthan, India, is among the largest royal residences in the world.** The palace, with 347 rooms, is the main residence of the former Jodhpur royal family, who have converted part of it into a museum. Its construction was done between 1929 and 1943 by Maharaja Umaid Singh. The palace complex is set in an area of 26 acres, with vast gardens. Among other rooms, it has a throne chamber, a meeting hall, a public audience hall, a banquet hall, dining halls, a ballroom, a library, a spa, a billiards room, four tennis courts, two squash courts and more. The inner vaulted dome, rising to 103 ft, is a major attraction in the palace.

328 **Many palaces have had an occupation makeover and are no longer mere royal residences.** The Palace of Westminster in London, UK, was built in the 16th century by Henry VIII, and today it houses the British Parliament. In

1870, the 1,100-room Houses of Parliament was rebuilt after a fire destroyed most of the original palace in 1834.

329 **One of the grandest palaces in Europe, the Palace of Versailles in France, was built in 1624.** A few kilometres out of Paris, it was from 1682 to 1715 the opulent and magnificent home of Louis XIV. Built originally by his father Louis XIII, it boasts of an amazing 240 ft chandelier in the 'Hall of Mirrors' with 357 mirrors. It has more than 5,000 pieces of exquisite furniture, 16,000 famous paintings and 400 sculptures. Capable of hosting up to 20,000 people at a time, it has 700 rooms, 2,000 windows, 1,250 chimneys, 67 staircases and 1,400 fountains.

Palace of Versailles

330 **Modelled on the palace at Versailles is the equally grand Peterhof Palace a few miles out of St. Petersburg in Russia, and now a museum and park.** Built between 1709 and1717, it is a spectacular gold and marble palace by the sea. With 144 fountains (one of which will spray you if you step on a particular tile) and 200 statues, it is set in decoratively laid gardens spread over 2,500 acres. It also has two massive cascading staircases from the palace to a giant statue of Samson wrestling with a lion.

331 **China's 15th century Forbidden City in Beijing, built of wood and massive stones, is the world's largest palace complex.** It is spread over 7,750,000 sq. ft, with 90 palace quarters and courtyards, 980 buildings and 8,000-

Forbidden City

odd rooms. Home to 24 emperors, it has rows and rows of statues of dragons, phoenixes, turtles and lions for good fortune. The Forbidden City was built by the 'ice lubrication' technique, according to ancient Chinese documents which describe how it took 28 days to transport a 123-tonne stone here from a quarry 70 km away by ice sledge in the winter. A path of ice was created along the roads and lubricated with water from wells dug alongside to help move the sledge pulled by teams of 46 men.

332 **The Royal Palace in Madrid, Spain, built in 1735, is the largest functioning royal palace in Europe.** With a floor area of 1,450,000 sq. ft and 3,418 rooms, 'Palacio Real' is the official residence of King Felipe V of Spain, but he doesn't live there anymore. Rich with paintings of famous artists, it is set among lovely large gardens and is at the service of the government.

Spain's Royal Palace

333 The **Grand Palace in Bangkok, Thailand, houses the famous Temple of the Emerald Buddha.** The Emerald Buddha traces its roots to India around 500 hundred years ago from where it was brought after the Lord

Buddha attained nirvana. It was enshrined in the Wat Phra Kaew temple within the palace grounds in 1782, when the palace was built during Rama I's reign. This is a 26 in seated meditating Buddha made of green emerald stone and clothed in gold.

334 **In the middle of Man Sagar Lake in Jaipur in Rajasthan, India, the Jal Mahal pops up from under the water unlike any other palace on a lake.** Made of red sandstone, four of its storeys (out of five) are under water and only the top floor is visible. The palace was built here when there was a drought. And once the lake filled up centuries later, it got submerged! It got a makeover during the rule of Raja Jai Singh II in the 18th century. After 300 years it was restored and reopened to host art exhibitions and interactive workshops.

335 **The Istana Nurul Iman palace in Brunei, covering an enormous 21,52,782 sq ft, is the largest residential palace in the world today.** Completed in January 1984, it has domes gilded with 22-carat gold, 1,788 rooms, 257 washrooms, gold-plated escalators, air-conditioned stables for the sultan's Argentine polo ponies and an 800-car underground garage. It also has a private museum displaying all the Formula One championship-winning race cars since 1980.

336 **The Palace of the Parliament in Bucharest, Romania, built by dictator Nicolae Ceausescu in 1986, is the world's largest non-residential palace in the world.** Under the Palace of the Parliament Bucharest, past eight underground levels, buried 33 feet below ground level is a steel door that leads to a small room just 269 square feet wide with 5 ft thick walls and fitted out with a powerful

337 **Its 98,000 dazzling bulbs light up Mysuru's night skies during the Dasara festival.** The three-storeyed fine grey granite Amba Vilas Palace in Karnataka, India, has a '*kalyana mandapa*' built entirely in Glasgow and transported here. Commissioned by Maharaja Krishnaraja Wodeyar IV and his mother in 1897 when the earlier palace burnt down, it was built between 1987 and 1912. A unique blend of Hindu, Mughal, Rajput and Gothic styles, it has a 145 ft five-storey tower, striking pink marble domes and a gallery of traditional dolls.

Inside Amba Vilas Palace

air filtering system. This is a nuclear bunker as Ceausescu feared nuclear war.

338 **Tibet is the seat of the spiritual leader Dalai Lama and Potala Palace is the highest ancient palace in the world, 12,300 ft above sea level and towering 300 ft above the city of Lhasa. Spread over 32 acres and 13 storeys high, it was built by the fifth Dalai Lama in 1645.**

Potala Palace

16

RESIDENCES OF HEADS OF STATE

The Head of State of a country, such as prime minister or a president, gets to live in a fabulous residence owned by the government of the country. Ambassadors in a foreign country often enjoy luxurious residences too.

339 **When India became independent, a fabulous palatial sandstone edifice designed and built by Edwin Lutyens for the British Viceroy in Delhi in 1929 became Rashtrapati Bhavan, the President of India's official residence.**

340 **Situated on top of Raisina Hill, amid lovely gardens – with some 100 varieties of flowers – Rashtrapati Bhavan looks towards India Gate, a memorial gateway-arch for martyred soldiers of the First World War.** At the end of the main hall, the Darbar Hall, there is a statue of the Buddha that dates to the 4th century. The statue is exactly on the same level as India Gate.

341 **Rashtrapati Bhavan in Delhi is spread over 320 acres and took 17 years to build.** It has more than 17.5 km

Rashtrapati Bhavan

of corridors, 340 rooms and 37 fountains. More than 29,000 workers were employed and 700 million bricks and 3,000,000 cu. ft of stone were used in its 200,000 sq. ft spread.

342 **Small lights above the portraits of former presidents in Rashtrapati Bhavan's banquet hall, which seats 140 guests at a time, silently signal to the staff when and when not to serve, or when to clear the hall. It also has a secret gallery for musicians to sit and play.**

343 **Home to all the US Presidents since 1800, The White House on 1600 Pennsylvania Avenue, Washington, DC, is also the President of the United States' office – in the West Wing.** Why is it called 'White House'? No one knows. Possibly because it was built with white-painted Aquia Creek sandstone – around 2,160 litres of paint is needed to cover just the outside. It was known simply as the 'Executive Mansion', until 26th president Theodore Roosevelt first referred to it as 'the white house' and the name stuck.

344 **The White House has six levels, 132 rooms and 32 bathrooms.** There are also 412 doors, 147 windows, 28 fireplaces, seven staircases and three elevators. It also has tennis courts, jogging tracks, swimming pools, a, billiard room, a bowling lane and a 3-D movie theatre. A trapdoor under the president's desk in the Oval Office leads to an underground command bunker.

The White House

345 **Overlooking the river Moskva in the centre of Moscow, Russia, is the 2nd century BCE site of the fortified complex of the Grand Palace Kremlin.** Designed and rebuilt between 1837 and 1849 by architect Konstantin Thon, the palace within this large fortress is home to the country's president.

346 **The five stars on top of the Kremlin weigh one tonne each and are made of ruby to enhance their shine. The total weight of clock and bells on top is 25 tonnes.**

347 **Number 10, Downing Street, in London, UK, is where the prime minister of the UK lives and works.** Though not a grand palace and technically not the residence of a head of state (the Queen is considered the actual head of state), it combines two mansions. It is over 300 years old and has about 100 rooms. The private residence is on the third floor and there is a kitchen in the basement. Visitors are not allowed.

348 **Larry, a male brown and white tabby cat, is the 10 Downing Street cat and is Chief Mouser to the Cabinet Office. This is the title of the official resident cat of the prime minister, whose main job is to officially hunt mice. There has been a resident cat at the address since the year 1515!**

349 **Originally designed by architect Sir Christopher Wren in 1687, number 10 Downing Street is a heavily guarded building.** Its public-facing door cannot be opened from the outside because it has no handle or latch.

350 Located in the City of Westminster in London, Buckingham Palace is the residence and main office of the British monarchy, since 1837. Queen Victoria, who

acceded to the throne that year, was the first monarch to reside there. Spread over almost 830,000 sq. ft, the palace has 775 rooms.

351 **The Turkish president's grand new residence, called Ak Saray (White Palace), built in 2014 in Ankara, displaced India's Rashtrapati Bhavan as the largest presidential residence in the world.** It has more than 1,000 rooms, four underground storeys and nearly 50 times the floor space of the White House. It covers an area of 3.2 million sq. ft.

352 **The Royal Palace of Madrid, the largest palace in Europe by floor area (1,453,128 sq. ft), is the official residence of the Spanish royal family.** However, they only use this palace, built on the site of a 9th century fortress, only for state ceremonies. The royal family lives in the less lavish Palacio de la Zarzuela.

353 **The Embassy of the United States of America in Baghdad, Iraq, with 104 acres, is the largest and most expensive embassy in the world. It is nearly as large as the Vatican, a country by itself.**

354 **The USA has a total of 271 embassy buildings spread across the world.** France and China come closest with

267 and 258, respectively. India isn't too far behind, with the 12th largest presence in the world and almost 175 diplomatic buildings, though some are rented.

355 **Overlooking the Spree River in Berlin, Germany, is one of the oldest presidential palaces in the world, the Bellevue Palace.** Built and designed by architect Michael Philipp Boumann in 1786 for a Prussian prince, it is also among the world's most beautiful head of state residences. With Corinthian pilasters and wings on either side, it is set among some lovely gardens in Tiergarten. It became the president's residence in 1994.

356 **Designed and built by architect Armand-Claude Mollet in 1722, the lavish Elysee Palace in Paris, France, in lilac and gold, has been the home of the presidents of the French Republic on and off since 1848.** Spread over 11,000 sq. ft, it has 369 rooms and an ornate wrought-iron gate at the back of its gardens, topped with a gilded rooster, the French national symbol.

357 **Located near the famous Avenue Champs-Elysees, the Elysee Palace has been constructed in the French classical style.** It's open to the public only once a year, during the European Heritage Days in mid-September.

358 **The Elysee Palace is luxurious.** It is said to have 6,500 pieces of tableware and 90 exquisite tablecloths. It also has 3,000 Baccarat crystal glasses, 2,000 bottles of grand-cru wines, 2,000 pieces of antique furniture, 200 magnificent tapestries and some 320 clocks. As many as 800 members of staff including 350 soldiers are always in attendance.

359 **Built in 1864, the Dar-al-Makhzen palace is the official and main residence of the king of Morocco.** When the country became independent in 1956, the kings chose this as the main palace. Its remarkable features are the large expanse of gardens, a French look (Morocco was a French colony) and traditional Arabic motifs.

360 **Located on the banks of the Brunei River, south of Bandar Seri Begawan, Brunei's capital, the Istana Nurul Iman is the official residence of the Sultan of Brunei.** The name is translated to mean 'the Palace of the Light of Faith'. It has nearly 1,800 rooms and a floor area of over 2 million sq. ft.

361 **The Palacio da Alvorada is the official seat of the president of Brazil and was built between 1957 and 1958.** It is one the most recent and modern residences for the head of state of a country. Designed by architect Oscar Niemeyer, it has a floor area of 79,000 sq. ft. There are three levels, and the ground floor has the entrance hall, waiting room, state room, library, mezzanine, dining room, music room and banquet room.

362 **The royal family of Belgium lives in the Castle of Laeken on the periphery of Brussels, though the Royal Palace of Brussels is their official palace and seat of administration.** It sits in a large park called the Royal Domain of Laeken and was originally called the Castle of Schonenberg. It was built during 1782–84, with many pavilions, including Chinese and Japanese ones.

An engraving of the Castle of Laeken (1827)

363 **Meaning 'The Pink House', Casa Rosada is the residence and office of the president of Argentina.** It also has a museum, with objects connected to former presidents of Argentina. It sits on the site of an earlier 16th century fort. It is said that one of the presidents, Domingo Sarmiento (in office: 1868–74), who had the building painted red to combine the red (Federalists) and white (Unitarians) colours of the country's two politically opposed parties.

364 **Located on the highest of the seven hills of Rome, the Quirinal Palace is the current official residence of the President of Italy.** With an enormous area of almost 1.2 million sq. ft, it is 20 times larger than the White House. Since its construction in 1583, it has housed 30 popes, four kings and 11 Italian presidents. Its gardens house a famous water organ, constructed between 1997

and 1999 by Barthelemy Formentelli, who followed the specifications of an earlier nineteenth century organ. The organ is fed by a waterfall and has a single keyboard of 41 notes.

365 **The Grand Palace in Bangkok, Thailand, has been the official residence of the Kings of Siam (and later Thailand) since 1782.** This rectangular-plan complex occupies nearly 2,350,000 sq. ft. The Thai monarch now resides at another palace, but the Grand Palace is still used for official events and ceremonies. It is currently partially open to the public as a museum, but also houses several royal offices.

366 **The Royal Palace of Amsterdam in the Netherlands was at first constructed to be used as a city hall in the 17th century!** This splendid building later became the palace of the Dutch Royal House.

17

SKYSCRAPERS

These engineering marvels stand astonishingly tall, weathering all storms without keeling over. There is something about skyscrapers that is awe-inspiring.

367 **The word skyscraper comes from a boat!** Skyscraper comes from a nautical term which refers to a small triangular sail placed above the skysail on a sailing ship. In the late nineteenth century, the term was first applied to tall buildings being constructed in Chicago and New York City.

Guaranty Building, USA

368 **The pioneer in skyscrapers was an American.** Louis Henry Sullivan (1856–1924) was an American architect, who has been called the 'father of skyscrapers'. The phrase 'form follows function' is attributed to him, although he credited the origin of the concept to an ancient Roman architect. Marcus

Vitruvius Pollio was an engineer and author, who first said in his book *De Architectura* that a structure must exhibit the three qualities of '*firmitas, utilitas, venustas*' – it must be 'solid, useful, beautiful'. Sullivan's over 100 works in collaboration with Dankmar Adler, during 1879–95, include the Auditorium Building, Chicago; the Guaranty Building, Buffalo, New York; and the Wainwright Building, St. Louis, Missouri.

369 **3 September is celebrated as 'Skyscraper Day' globally as it is the birthday of groundbreaking skyscraper architect Louis Henry Sullivan.**

370 **The first skyscraper had only ten storeys.** William Le Baron Jenney was an American architect who, it is said, saw his wife place a heavy book on top of a small bird cage. It didn't topple over nor did it shake. It balanced perfectly. An iron skeletal frame the architect thought to himself – lighter than stone and easier to frame – could perhaps easily hold up a whole building. And the idea for the world's first iron skyscraper was born. By then a new metal made its appearance: steel. It revolutionized the building industry. And the 138 ft, ten-storeyed Home Insurance Building in Chicago, built in 1885, became the world's first steel-frame skyscraper.

371 **The Eiffel Tower was the tallest structure in the world till 1930.** The 1,046 ft Chrysler Building in New York City was the first building that overtook the Eiffel Tower as the tallest structure in the world. Built in 1930, its 180 ft sunburst-patterned stainless steel spire has stainless steel automobile icons like radiator caps in the form of 'Mercury' in a frieze at the base of the tower. In 1931 the Empire State Building surpassed it in height.

372 How high was high?

In the early 1900s, steel-frame buildings had to be a minimum of 10 storeys high to be officially termed 'skyscrapers'. With the 'Chicago school of architecture' and the discovery of steel, buildings spread upwards beyond the clouds instead of sideways and changed the skylines of many cities in the USA. Those following this school of architecture led the use of the new technologies of steel-frame construction in commercial buildings. It also set off a race between Chicago and New York to see who could build the highest building ever.

Today, to be officially called a skyscraper, the building has to have a continuous high-rise building that is more than 40 storeys high and 492 ft tall, be habitable, have mechanical means of upward transportation, be fire-resistant, and to withstand the lateral forces of wind and earthquakes. Skyscrapers over 165 ft high or 14 storeys high are categorized as 'Tall'; those that are 984 ft and above are 'Supertall'; and buildings above 1,968 ft are called 'Megatall'.

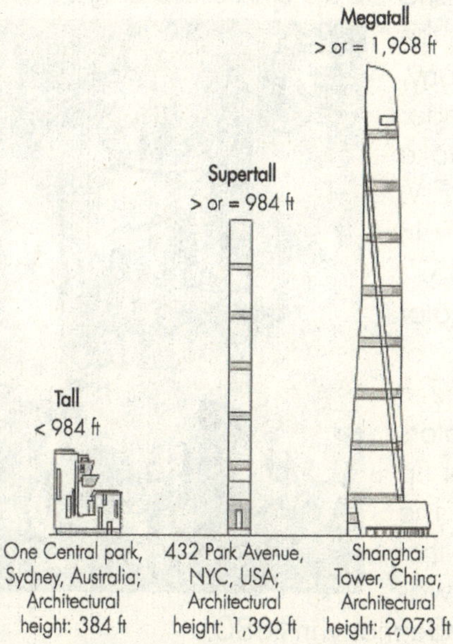

373 **The first building in the world to touch 100 floors was the Empire State Building in New York, USA.** This skyscraper has 102 storeys and took only 410 days to complete in 1931. Designed by a company called Shreve, Lamb & Harmon, it is 1,250 ft tall. Called 'Empire State' after New York's nickname, it was the tallest in the world for 40 years till the twin towers of the 1,368 ft World Trade Centre were built in 1972 (these were later destroyed in the 9/11 terrorist attacks). The Empire State Building was built with 10 million bricks, and has 6,514 windows 1,872 steps and 73 elevators. A race up its stairs to the 86th floor is held every year, with a total of 1,576 steps. It has a 'secret' 103rd floor. The building is said to be struck by lightning an average of 23 times a year.

374 **Elevator alert!** Elisha Otis, founder of the Otis Elevator Company, installed the first passenger safety device – the brake – in an elevator in the E.V. Haughwout Building in New York, USA, in 1857. At the time, that elevator was only capable of travelling at a mere 0.67 ft per second. Now elevators can move at a speed of up to 54.6 ft per second. The first electric elevator that could control speed was installed by Siemens in Germany in1880.

Elisha Otis demonstrating the elevator

375 **Built in 1972 in just 30 days, the Nakagin Capsule Tower in Tokyo, Japan, is an unusual one.** This 14-storey, mixed-use residential and office tower, designed by architect Kisho Kurokawa, consists of 140 individual capsule units connected together by two concrete towers. Like laundry baskets stacked one upon the other, each capsule is 107 sq. ft and connected to the core by four high-tension bolts. This first example of capsule architecture is now dilapidated.

376 **There's a skyscraper called the Shard.** When a 95-storey skyscraper was proposed in 2009 for the Southwark area of London in a development project, there was much opposition to it. English Heritage, a charity that manages over 400 historic monuments, buildings and places, said it would be 'a shard of glass through the heart of historic London'. But its Italian architect, Renzo Piano, imagined it to reflect the history of London, its church steeples and railway lines. At 309.6 m (1,016 ft) at its highest point, the Shard, completed in 2012, is the tallest building in the UK, the tallest building in the European Union, and the fifth-tallest building in Europe.

377 **There was an 'Einstein of skyscrapers'!** Fazlur Khan, a Bangladeshi–American engineer, came up with innovative tube structures to build skyscrapers for the first time. It helped buildings become even lighter and higher and take on any shape. They didn't have to be rectangular boxes any longer. He is famous for his 100-storey and 1,128 ft high John Hancock/875 North Michigan Avenue Tower built in 1969 and the 108-storey and 1,451 ft high Sears (now Willis) Tower built in 1974.

378 **Skyscrapers are ranked by their architectural height.** A height calculator estimates the height of skyscrapers from the level of the lowest, significant, open-air, pedestrian entrance to the architectural top of the building, including spires, but not including antennae, signages, flag poles or other functional equipment.

379 **What is the tallest building in the world?** The Burj Khalifa, Dubai. At 2,717 ft, it is in the shape of a Hymenocallis desert flower. If laid end to end, it can stretch a quarter of the way round the world! Imagine the weight of a hundred thousand elephants! – that's the amount of concrete used for it and the aluminum is equal to a Boeing 380 aircraft. Built in 2010, it has 163 habitable floors, above which are 46 floors that serve as a base for the spire of the building, which adds up to 209 floors. The highest occupied floor is at the 154th floor, and there are three observation decks at the 124th, 125th and 148th floors.

380 **The greenest skyscraper is not about its colour!** Built in 2014 at 1,671 ft, the Taipei 101 (it has that many floors) was the tallest and largest green building in the world till 2011. It was also the first building in the world to break the half-kilometre mark in height. It has a massive gold-coloured iron wind damper that keeps the tower stable through typhoons and earthquakes. Its green features include its glazed structural facade with double-pane windows, providing heat and UV protection. Air units draw in air to lower the carbon dioxide levels.

381 **Ooh... feel it sway.** Scary though it may seem, skyscrapers sway in storms. It's apparently all right for skyscrapers to sway 2 to 5 ft this way and that. An in-built

mechanical counterweight to factor in the force of wind or an earthquake keeps them standing.

'Turning Torso'

382 **Ever seen a skyscraper that turns and twists?** 'Turning Torso' in Malmo in Sweden is a white marble 'twisting' residential skyscraper built in 2001 by Santiago Calatrava. At 190 m, it is not only the tallest building in Sweden but also the first twisted skyscraper in the world. Nine box units each of five floors set around a steel support form a spiral structure that mimics a stationary twisting human spine!

383 **The 'grandfather of skyscrapers' is the Flax Mill in Shrewsbury, UK.** This five-storey, 18th century building from 1797 had cast iron beams and columns, from which the idea of converting to steel perhaps took off.

384 **To be considered a building, at least 50 per cent of its height must be occupiable.** Telecommunications or observation towers that do not meet this condition are not included in the 'tallest' lists of the Council on Tall Buildings and Urban Habitat (CTBUH), an international organisation, considered the authority on tall buildings and sustainable urban design, in Chicago, Illinois, USA.

385 **Here's a concrete example of a record.** The 87-storey Lakhta Center in St. Petersburg, Russia, rises to 1,516 ft. The tallest building in Russia, it has an amphitheatre with 2,000 seats, a 357-m high observation point, a pedestrian mall and a water park. The concrete pouring of the bottom slab of its foundation was registered by Guinness World Records as the largest continuous concrete pour.

386 **A skyscraper that opens bottles?** Designed by American architect Kohn Pedersen Fox, the Shanghai World Financial Center is a supertall skyscraper in the Pudong district, Shanghai, China. It houses offices, conference rooms, observation decks, hotels and malls. Its most unusual feature is the trapezoid 'hole' at the top, to lower wind pressure. It's popularly called the 'bottle opener' and bottle-opener souvenirs that look like it are sold in its gift shop.

Shanghai World Financial Center

387 **Till 2011, the tallest residential building was in Australia.** The 80-storey Queensland Number 1 lost that title to the Marina Torch in Dubai in 2011. Today it is the sixth tallest in the world and the tallest in Australia. Built in 2005 in the shape of an Olympic torch, it is 1,058 ft high and has 527 spacious residences.

388 **The Jeddah Tower in the UAE is daring to go where no building has gone before – beyond 1 km! It will have 167 floors above ground when complete in 2020.**

389 **Go round and round.** The world's first prefabricated rotating tower that twists and turns will be the Dynamic Tower Dubai. David Fischer designed the moving 1,378 ft, 80-floor tower in such a way that the floors in it can rotate 360 degrees in both directions and allow each tenant to see different views from their apartment windows. A special elevator at the concrete core of the tower will enable residents to park their car right next to their apartments!

18

SYNAGOGUES

Different communities of Jews use different names for their place of worship – *beyt knesset* (house of assembly), *shul* (close to 'school'), *kal* (community), *sinagoga, esnoga, kenis* or simply temple. The Greek-origin word *synagogue* is used in English to include all these.

390 **The word 'synagogue' comes from the Greek word '*sunagogue*' meaning a house of gathering.** Usually of two floors, it has a large hall with the Holy Ark (an ornamental closet containing the Jewish holy book, the Torah), and the 'Bima' (a raised platform for the person to read the Torah). The Bima will either be in the middle of the hall or in front of the Ark. The Ark always faces Jerusalem.

391 **The oldest synagogue was built where a young brave girl died.** Legend goes that a Jewish girl fled from the land of Israel carrying with her a stone from the Temple of Jerusalem and a Torah scroll. On reaching the island of Djerba in Tunisia she collapsed and died. And on that spot was built the El Ghriba or the Djerba

Djerba Synagogue

Synagogue. There is a niche within, known as 'Magrath Sibiya' or 'the cave of the girl' just below the ornamental Holy Ark. The El Ghriba was first built either in 586 BCE or in 70 CE and has been in continuous use since. Its main hall with rows of arches, originally had twelve windows but now have more. Its inner walls are covered with lovely blue and white glazed tiles with decorative eight-sided patterns. The Djerba Synagogue has had a number of terrorist attacks.

392 **The number 12 is important to the Jewish people and considered holy.** It denotes the 12 tribes of Israel from whom they are descended. It will always figure somewhere or the other as an architectural feature in synagogues, such as with 12 windows, 12 stained-glass panels and so on.

393 **Built in the Gothic style, the design of the Old New Synagogue of Prague in the Czech Republic is the oldest surviving synagogue in Europe.** It incorporates vines and bunches of grapes at the entrance in clusters of 12. It also has narrow gothic windows on the inside again symbolizing the number twelve. Built in 1270 from the stones of King Solomon's temple, it contains the 'Golem of Prague.' When the Jews were being persecuted in the 16th century, one of their rabbis, through prayers, magically created an animated figure out of mud with inscriptions on its forehead – a 'golem' which is said to have protected them. Later divested of its powers because it turned uncontrollable, it was sealed in an attic forever. It is still there, they say, in a mysterious locked room at the synagogue.

394 **There are about 20,000 synagogues in the world.** Some 10,000 are in Israel alone. About 3,727 are in

395 **Designed by architects Dezso Jakab and Marcell Komor and built in 1902 the Subotica Synagogue, Serbia, was one of the first buildings to use concrete and steel, edged with decorative red brick and terracotta tiles.** Located near the Serbia–Hungary border, and built in the stunning Art Nouveau style, it was restored as recently as March 2018. It has a large gilded eight-sided dome with a multicoloured tiled roof. Orange and gold inside, it is surrounded by smaller domes with the Star of David on them.

the USA, with another 1,000 in the rest of the Americas. There are close to 3,500 in Europe and Asia, with a few more scattered around the rest of the world.

396 **The largest synagogue in the world is in Israel.** The Belz Great Synagogue in Jerusalem is simply huge. Built in 2000, its enormous hall can seat 10,000 people for prayer at a time and is a magnificent re-creation of the original Belz Synagogue in the Ukrainian town of Belz, which was

equally big but was destroyed during the Holocaust. The Israeli Belz, which took 15 years to build, has no fewer than nine chandeliers made out of 200,000 Czechoslovakian crystals and a large exquisitely decorated wooden Ark. Usually Arks are about five to six metres high but the Belz Holy Ark is12 m high, weighs 18 tonnes, and can hold 70 Torah scrolls.

397 **Built in 1906 and named in honour of Emperor Franz Joseph I of Austria's silver jubilee, the Jubilee Synagogue in Prague in the Czech Republic is a museum today.** Designed by architect Wilhelm Stiassny, this colourful building has a red and gold facade featuring a rosette window surrounded by blue. A mixture of Art Nouveau and Moorish styles catches the eye, along with its amazing blue horseshoe arches.

Jubilee Synagogue

398 **The Ben Ezra synagogue of Cairo was earlier a Christian church.** It was bought by Ben Ezra, one of the great rabbis of the Jews, for 20,000 dinars from the Christians who could not to pay the taxes imposed on them by the Muslim rulers of the time. This building from 882 CE has a Star of David in the centre of the ceiling and is decorated in Turkish and Roman styles with geometric and floral patterns. It has an octagonal Bima, rows of marble columns, and pearl and ivory mosaics on which are engraved words of the Torah in Hebrew. Strangely, the names of three Muslim caliphs and a Mamluk sultan are also inscribed in Arabic on the chandeliers.

399 **The Dohany Street Synagogue in Budapest, Hungary, is the largest synagogue in Europe and the second largest in the world.** The structure is 246 ft long and 88.5 ft wide, and seats nearly 3,000 people. Designed by Austrian architect Ludwig Forster, it has a lovely rose window above the front door with windows on either side, said to resemble the two tablets on which Moses wrote the Ten Commandments. The Moorish architectural touch is evident in its brickwork and two onion-topped towers. The complex includes a cemetery, a museum, a Heroes' Temple for World War Hungarian Jewish martyrs, and a memorial park with a silver sculpture of a weeping willow whose leaves bear the names of 400,000 Hungarian Jews who were victims of the Holocaust.

400 **The Ohel Jakob or Jacob's Tent Synagogue in Munich, Germany, is a very modern building.** It consists of two cubes, one on top of the other. The bottom one in stone represents the 'Wailing Wall' in Jerusalem, and the top cube is in glass with interlaced Stars of David sheathed in a bronze metal veil. Built to replace the old synagogue destroyed in 1938 by the Nazis, it is modern, clean and airy with gold Hebrew lettering on the inside walls. It is connected to the community centre further away by a 'Corridor of Remembrance' that bears the names of more than 5,000 Jews killed during the Holocaust.

401 **Three impressive horseshoe arches welcome you at the entrance of the grand Great Synagogue of Florence, Italy.** Onion-shaped copper domes atop more horseshoe-arched towers with a smooth marble façade complete it. Built in 1882 by architects Mariano Falcini, Professor

Vincente Micheli and Marco Treves, it boasts of gold-plated motifs, exquisite inlaid marble floors, rich mosaics and stained-glass windows that are Moorish in style.

402 **With its grand 154 m high cupola and lovely pink colouring, the Grand Choral Synagogue in St. Petersburg, Russia, is among the largest synagogues in Europe.** Designed lavishly by architect Vasily Stasov in 1893 and renovated in 2003, it can seat about 1,200 people. Its stained-glass windows and decorative arches are eye-catching. The door is opened by a special silver key and its exquisite Ark is large enough to contain 7 Torah scrolls. Above all, it is known for its astounding acoustics. If you whisper softly into a wall at one end of the hall, the words will carry perfectly across 32 ft to the other end of the hall – and sound amplified in the centre of the hall.

403 **Simple and humble, there is the little Etz Haim Synagogue in Athens, Greece, meaning 'Tree of Life.'** Built in 1904, it has in its courtyard a palm tree that is more than 100 years old.

404 **The Paradesi ('foreigner') Synagogue is one of seven synagogues in Kochi in Kerala, India, and the oldest one in use among the Commonwealth of Nations.** Built in 1567 by Spanish Jews in Cochin, it features amazing hand-painted bright blue willow

Paradesi Synagogue

porcelain tiles from China on its floors, sparkling Belgium crystal chandeliers, a shining brass railed Bima and an Ark in carved teakwood that contains four scrolls of the Torah in gold and silver casing. This synagogue also has some 4th-century copper plates engraved in Malayalam and gold crowns gifted by the rulers of Cochin and Travancore, besides an exquisite rug from Ethiopian ruler Haile Selassie. It is also the only synagogue in the world where you have to leave your footwear outside just like at other Indian places of worship!

405 **Commissioned by Sir Jacob Sassoon, the descendant of an Iraqi Jewish business family settled in Mumbai, the Knesset Eliyahoo Synagogue in Colaba, Mumbai, has just been renovated and opened for worship.** Built in 1884, with its Minton tile floors from England, Burmese teak furnishings and Victorian stained-glass windows, it has an ornately carved marbled Bima with a tall, stained-glass arch that reaches the ceiling. The stained-glass windows have oranges, pomegranates and roses painted on them. All the painted items are allowed as offering in the synagogue.

Temple of Freedom Synagogue

406 **The Ark in a synagogue always faces towards Jerusalem, where the original temple of the Jews stood during Jesus's time. And above the Ark, there is always a lit lamp called the 'eternal light'.**

407 **Built in 1932, the Templo Libertad or the Temple of Freedom Synagogue in Buenos Aires, Argentina, is a national monument.** It has an impressively large Star of David in front, below a stone arch. A high ceiling

with a beautiful chandelier and unusually lovely wooden seats make this one of the loveliest synagogues in the Americas. It also houses a rare Walcker pipe organ.

408 **The Ohr Torah Synagogue in Acre, Tunisia, is completely clad in colourful mosaics.** Modelled on the ancient El Ghriba synagogue, the mosaics trace the story and history of the Jewish people. Built in 1955, it has seven Arks and 140 stained-glass windows.

Mosaic in Ohr Torah Synagogue

409 **Built in 1878, the Great Synagogue of Sydney, Australia, is one of the finest buildings in the city.** With a large rose window and columns, it has magnificent cast-iron gates, elaborate stone carvings and a grand gold-starred dark blue ceiling. Designed by architect Thomas Rowe, it is a mixture of Gothic, Byzantine and Romanesque styles.

410 **Synagogues have a main sanctuary for prayer and often also have smaller rooms for study.** Some have a separate room for Torah study, called the *beth midrash* (house of study).

411 **The Soho Synagogue in New York City looks nothing like a conventional synagogue inside or outside.** It has a Star of David at the front, no doubt, but with modern art on its brick walls, open pipes and a steel-and-glass stairwell. Its Ark is a round arc with overlapping circles that slide open and close, with triangles that form the Star of David when they are closed on top of one another. It is a synagogue with a modern touch.

19

TEMPLES

The word temple comes from the Latin word *templum*, which means a sacred place used for prayer or rituals. Here are some fascinating temples, including Greek, Hindu, Buddhist, Jain and Sikh ones.

412 **A lake with waters from 151 rivers; 20,000 statues of Hindu Gods; 200 sculpted stone figures of monks and deities on its walls, and a 3,000 feet long red stone *parikrama* in the shape of a garland – how much more elaborate could it get?** There is also the 1,070 ft long Gajendra *peeth* (frieze) in pink sandstone with some 148 life-sized elephant sculptures, and those of 42 birds as well. The 100-acre complex, surrounding the 141 ft high, 316 ft wide and 356 ft long Akshardham Temple, dedicated to Swami Laxminarayan, it also has some 108 faces of cows that represent 108 Hindu gods.

413 **Spread over 156 acres is the largest temple in India, the Ranganathaswamy Temple of Srirangam, Tamil Nadu.** With a 236 ft high gopuram and a gold vimana or crown in the shape of an 'Om', it is dedicated to Lord Vishnu, seen here in a reclining pose. Sometime in 1311, the story goes, the Delhi Sultanate under Alauddin Khilji plundered Srirangam and carried away the idol to give to his daughter. Dressed as musicians, priests then went to

Delhi, performed before the sultan and persuaded him to return it. But the daughter was inconsolable, so the sultan mounted a massive battle in 1323 and the idol was spirited away to Tirupati – until the victory of the Vijayanagar Empire in 1378 when the idol was reinstalled in the rebuilt temple. The massive temple has 21 towers and 39 pavilions with inscriptions on the walls that recount its restoration over the years. It has many exquisitely carved mandapams or halls including a 1,000-pillared granite one. With 50 other temples and nine ponds within it, it is one of the largest religious complexes in the world.

414 **Said to be built by Arjuna of the Pandavas is the Tungnath Temple, the highest Shiva temple in the world.** Discovered by Adi Shankaracharya in present-day Uttarakhand, India, among the Himalayan peaks some 1,000 years ago, the 12,467 ft high *shivalinga* is in black rock. It is one of the Panch Kedar or five Shiva temples built by the Pandavas, looking to atone for having killed their cousins in the Mahabharata war. Reluctant to see them, legend goes, Shiva went into hiding and distributed his body parts in five different locations. The Pandavas discovered each of them and built a temple over it.

415 **The prasad at a Kali Temple in Kolkata, India, run by the Chinese residents of Tangra, includes noodles, chop suey and fried rice.**

416 **Believe it or not, there is a temple where alcohol is offered to the deity.** Lord Shiva sits in the form of a fierce man with a garland of skulls around his neck in the Kal Bhairav Temple in Varanasi, Uttar Pradesh, India, where devotees are also given wine as prasad.

417 **A stunning 9th century masterpiece of exquisite Hindu architecture outside India is dedicated to the Trimurti or Trinity of Brahma the creator, Vishnu the preserver and Shiva the destroyer.** Time stands still at the intricately carved temples of Prambanan in Indonesia. A 154 ft high temple houses a 10 ft tall Shiva idol and relief sculptures that narrate the story of the Ramayana. The Vishnu temple stands tall at 108 ft with relief sculptures that tell you the story of Lord Krishna. The 108 ft tall Brahma temple continues the Ramayana stories. There are also four rows of 224 identical, concentrically arranged shrines in this massive complex, built by the Mataram rulers of Java, with temples dedicated to Shiva's bull Nandi, Brahma's swan Hamsa and Vishnu's mount Garuda.

418 **Founded by Swami Vivekananda in 1897, the Belur Math in Kolkata, West Bengal, India, is also the Ramakrishna Mission headquarters.** Spread over 40 acres, the temple complex in sandstone is dedicated to Sri Ramakrishna Paramahansa and his relics are kept inside. With symbols of different religions on its gates, the *math* is a stunning symbol of religious harmony, with its unique blend

of architectural elements like scalloped arches and lattice-filled horseshoes, lotuses and elephants.

419 **The Baha'i temple in New Delhi, India, is the only lotus-shaped temple in the world. It has 27 free-standing marble-covered 'petals' arranged in clusters of three to form nine sides, and a capacity of 2500 people.**

420 **Spread over 500 acres is the largest Hindu-turned-Buddhist temple in the world.** The Angkor Wat or the City of Temples, depicted on the flag of Cambodia, was dedicated to Vishnu and consists of hundreds of temples. Built by Khmer king Suryavarman II in the 12th century, the main temple is three storeys high and has a 10 ft 5.9 in tall sandstone statue of Lord Vishnu. With scenes from the Ramayana and Mahabharata on its walls, it also houses hundreds of Buddha statues as well. A moat, 650 ft wide and 13 ft deep, runs around this monument. It took more than 1,000 elephants, 3,00,000 workers, five million tonnes worth of sandstone and 35 years to build. The film *Lara Croft: Tomb Raider* was also shot here.

Angkor Wat, drawing (c. 1860)

421 **The Bullet Baba Mandir or Om Banna temple has a motorbike as its deity.** Near Jodhpur in Rajasthan, India, there is a temple dedicated to the motorcycle of one Om Singh Rathore who crashed his bike against a tree and died. The story goes that though the bike was repeatedly taken away and chained at a police station, it would end

up at the crash site and nobody knew how. So finally the bike was left at the crash site permanently. It soon turned into a 'bike' temple with hundreds of devotees turning up every day to pray for a safe journey. The motorcycle is a 350cc Royal Enfield Bullet-RNJ 7773.

422 **Where Shiva is said to have wed Parvati on the banks of the river Vaigai in Madurai, Tamil Nadu, stands the awe-inspiring 6th century Madurai Meenakshi Temple.** It is dedicated to Parvati in the form of Meenakshi and Shiva in the form of Sundreshwaran. This event is celebrated annually in April with hordes of pilgrims descending on the grand temple. Destroyed in wars in the 14th century, it was rebuilt during the Vijayanagar Empire in the 16th century. It is known for its enormously wide corridors, multistorey gopurams with exquisite animal carvings and the mandapam or hall with a thousand pillars, which make music when tapped.

Meenakshi Temple

423 **The cave temple of Parashurama, Indra and Surya in Bhaje in Maharashtra, India, built in 400 BCE, is considered to be the first and oldest 'temple' in India.**

424 **One of the oldest temples in the world may have been dedicated to the Dog Star or Sirius, the brightest star in the sky.** At Gobekli Tepe in southern Turkey is an 11,000-year-old site with round enclosures and rings of T-shaped stone pillars with carvings of fierce foxes, lions, scorpions and vultures. This is believed to be temple of Sirius, a star in the Canis Major or 'Greater Dog' constellation.

425 **The first known temple in the world was built by King Solomon in 10th century BCE on Temple Mount in the old city of Jerusalem. It was dedicated to the god Yahweh.**

426 **The oldest and the largest temple complex in Egypt is Karnak, meaning 'most select of places', and dedicated to Gods Amun, Mut and Khonsu.** Built and expanded from 2055 BCE to around 100 CE by nearly 30 pharaohs, it has many temples, massive sphinxes, towering pillars and about 134 giant columns. It also has the Great Hypostyle Hall large enough to fit in the Notre dame cathedral of France. It houses 5,000 statues of the King of Gods, Amun-Ra, and a 97 ft obelisk weighing 323 tonnes. Engravings of scalpels, forceps, prescriptions, medicine bottles and a Nilometer that measures water in the Kom Ombo temple here are even more startling.

427 **Built by Pharaoh Ramesses II in 1244 BCE to celebrate his victory in the battle of Kadesh, the famous Abu Simbel Temples took 20 years to construct.** Cut out of the solid rock of a cliff side, the two massive temples dedicated to Ramesses II and his queen Nefertari contain many statues, pillars, carvings and rock paintings. Four gigantic statues of a seated pharaoh Ramesses, each about

69 ft, grace the entrance of the larger temple and are built in such a way that on two days in a year – 22 October and 22 February – his birthday and the day of his coronation, the sun's rays fall directly on the Pharaoh and two other statues seated on a bench inside.

Abu Simbel Temples

428 **When the Aswan High Dam was built on the Nile River in the 1960s, it created Lake Nasser, a massive artificial water reservoir that everyone feared would flood the Abu Simbel Temples.** So in an amazing feat of engineering the two whole temples were cut into 1,035 blocks each of 20 to 30 tonnes. The four huge statues of the seated Ramesses II, and six more of him standing up, were sawn into pieces. These were all then lifted by cranes to their new home on a cliff 210 feet away from the dam and reassembled exactly as they were.

429 **For around 3,000 years nobody had known about the Abu Simbel Temples, covered in shifting sand, when a young boy called Abu Simbel happened to stumble upon them.** In 1813, he led Jean-Louis Burckhardt, a Swiss researcher, to it. Burckhardt managed to spot the top of a frieze in the shifting sands, brought in Egyptologist Giovanni Battista Belzoni and they found a way in.

430 **Built in 440 BCE, the Temple of Poseidon once boasted of a huge bearded marble statue of the Greek sea**

god. He, who is said to have masterminded earthquakes and controlled the seas, is now under lock and key in the National Archaeological Museum in Athens, Greece. Poseidon's famous and imposing statue is no longer there, but 15 of some 34 spectacular Doric marble columns in his massive temple look out into the Aegean Sea in southern Greece.

Temple of Hercules

431 **Looking down on Amman, the capital of Jordan, are the remnants of the rather unusual Temple of Hercules.** Built by a Roman governor during the time of Marcus Aurelius (162–66 CE), it has three humongous fingers, an elbow and a spread of round marble chips. These fingers with their well-manicured nails are deemed to be what is left of the enormous statue of the powerfully strong Roman God Hercules, who could single-handedly slay wild beasts and demons.

432 **A shining example of Roman architectural excellence is the Pantheon of Rome.** Built in 126 CE, it was a temple for all Roman gods. Converted into a church in the 7th century, it has the world's largest unsupported dome with an amazing oculus or hole on top through which the sun lights up the whole temple. Sixteen massive granite columns support the round portico and a fountain in front while an obelisk of Ramses II and four dolphins decorate its base.

433 **Stone for the Corinthian pillars of the Pantheon, each of them weighing 60 tonnes, came from Egypt.** They were first brought from the quarries about 160 km away on wooden sleds to the River Nile, after which they

were floated down the river on barges when water levels were high. They were then shifted to boats to cross the Mediterranean Sea to the port of Ostia and put back again on barges and pulled up the river Tiber into Rome.

Golden Temple (1880)

434 The 16th century Sri Harmandir Sahib gurudwara or the Golden Temple in Amritsar in Punjab, India, is built with marble and many parts of it, including the dome, are covered in gold.

435 **You can tell the time by just looking at this temple.** Built by King Narasimhadeva I during 1243–55 CE and dedicated to the sun god, the famous Sun Temple of Konark in Odisha, India, is in the form of an enormous chariot with 24 exquisitely carved wheels, shown to be pulled by seven rearing horses. Forming sundials, the shadows cast by the spokes of the wheels tell the exact time at any time of day. It took 1,200 men 12 years to build this architectural marvel.

436 **Stupas, pagodas and wats are types of Buddhist sacred spaces.** Pagodas are typically in the form of a many-tiered tower while stupas are mound-like structures containing Buddhist relics. Wats are Buddhist temple complexes.

437 **The oldest Buddhist shrine is a 6th century wooden structure in Lumbini, Nepal, the birthplace of Gautam Buddha.** Radiocarbon and luminescence techniques confirm the possibility of it dating back to 550 BCE. Lumbini was where Gautama Buddha was born.

438 The young Prince Gautama, seeing the suffering of people, left his home, palace and kingdom in

Kapilavastu (in present-day Nepal) in search of a solution. Reaching Gaya in Bihar he sat under a peepul tree and meditated. On the third day he attained 'enlightenment.' Emperor Ashoka of the Mauryan Empire built the Mahabodhi Temple around that tree (which still exists) 250 years later and dedicated it to the Buddha. He also built a Vajrasana, a 'diamond throne', below the tree on the spot where he believed Buddha attained 'Maha Bodhi' or great enlightenment.

439 **The Buddha spent seven weeks in the Mahabodhi Temple surroundings contemplating the enlightenment he had experienced, and there is something to indicate each event.** The first week, he spent meditating under the peepul or 'Bodhi' tree, which marks that spot. The second week, he stood and stared fixedly at the same tree, and this is marked by an 'Animeshlocha' or 'unblinking stupa' and a statue of Buddha staring at the tree. The third week, he went to and back from the tree to the unblinking stupa, and lotus blooms mark the path. The fourth week is marked by a stupa, the 'Ratnagar Chaitya', and the fifth week, which he spent under another tree is marked by King Ashoka's engraved pillar. The sixth week, he spent by a lotus pond where his footprints can be seen and the seventh week, under a Rajyatna tree. All these go to make this 11.2-acre spread a very sacred site for Buddhists.

440 **A yellow sandstone Buddha in a glass case graces the inside of the two-storey high main Mahabodhi Temple.** Its 180 ft high shikhara or tower, filled with niches, arches and carvings, is surrounded by four identical but smaller temples topped by umbrella-shaped domes. The temple, rebuilt many times in the past, was rediscovered from under layers of sand in the 19th century and restored by the British.

441 **The largest Buddhist temple complex in the world, the Borobudur Temple in Java, Indonesia, lay hidden for centuries.** Buried under volcanic ash from Mount Merapi and overgrown with vegetation, it was discovered in 1814 by the then British Lt Governor of Java, Sir Thomas Stamford Raffles and surprised the world by its size and beauty. The inscriptions on the now restored 8th century temple (113 ft tall, with its base measuring 403 x 403 ft) tell us that it took 75 years to complete. It features six square and three circular platforms capped by a central dome with 2,672 relief panels spread over its walls and 504 Buddha statues. The teachings of Buddha are inscribed and depicted on its surfaces. Seventy-two seated Buddhas in open bell-shaped stupas surround the 32.5 foot central dome. Two million stone blocks from nearby rivers, cut to size and transported to a rock hill 265 m above sea level, and placed without mortar were used build it.

Sandstone railings that surround the brick temple as well as the Bo tree are what remain of its original structure.

442 **The Kyaiktiyo Pagoda in Mon State, Myanmar, is a small pagoda built on top of a granite boulder 3,609 ft above the sea level with golden leaves pasted on it by**

Kyaiktiyo Pagoda

male devotees. Legend has it that the 24 ft high glittering rock, perched on a hillside, is balanced on a strand of Buddha's hair.

443 **The fabulous 326 ft high bell-shaped Shwedagon Pagoda in Yangon, Myanmar, is said to be at least 2,600 years old.** It features about 8,688 sheets of gold, 5,448 diamonds, 2,317 rubies, 13,153 gold bars, 1,065 golden bells, countless sapphires, hundreds of topaz and, at the very top, a single 72-carat diamond with a massive emerald that sparkles when the rays of the sun hit it.

444 **Ta Prohm in Siem Reap, Cambodia, looks almost as if the forests have swallowed it.** Made famous by the 'Tomb Raider' movies, this is where Angelina Jolie as Lara Croft picks up a flower and falls through the earth. This Buddhist temple was built in 1186 by Jayavarman III. With massive 100-year-old trees sprouting roots and leaves, moss-covered floors and giant creepers hanging from its huge uneven roofs, it is a popular tourist destination. It seems it even has a small carving of something that looks like a Stegosaurus, or a pangolin, or a lizard! No one is sure.

445 **The Great Sanchi Stupa in Madhya Pradesh is one of the oldest Buddhist stone structures in India and the largest stupa in the country.** With its railings, towers, pillars, and terraces symbolizing various aspects of Buddhist beliefs it is also the largest stupa in India. Built by Emperor Ashoka in 3rd century BCE, it was rediscovered and restored by the British in the 19th century.

446 **An unusual ornamental tower gracing London's skyline is the 164 ft high, ten-roofed Pagoda in Kew Gardens.** It was built in 1761 by architect William Chambers, who was inspired by dragon-decorated pagodas in China. It once had eighty, 250 kg dragons on its roof all made of solid pine till severe cold caused them to integrate. Now restored in lightweight nylon and painted in green, red, blue and silver, they weigh a mere 12 kg each.

447 **Built in the 7th century by Emperor Shomu the Todaiji Temple in Japan was an enormous wooden building 288 ft long and 169 ft wide.** It was once one of the powerful Seven Great Temples of Japan. Restored in 1980, it is among the largest wooden buildings in the world and home to a 53 ft high bronze statue of the Buddha, the largest in the world.

448 **In Anuradhapura, an ancient heritage city in Sri Lanka, is the 4th century stupa of Jetavanaramaya, the tallest and largest stupa in the world at 400 ft.** It is made up of 93.3 million baked bricks with a base area of 2,508,000 sq. ft.

449 **Clinging precariously to the cliff side of Datong in China is the Hanging Temple, dedicated to Buddhism, Taoism and Confucianism.** It has 40 rooms built on rock sides 89 ft above ground and are connected by an amazing labyrinth of passages. Built by

Hanging Temple

a monk named Liao Ran in the 4th century, it is kept in place by wooden crossbeams fixed on to the cliffs and is on the list of the top ten most dangerous structures in the world. Restored in the 1900s, it has some 78 statues and carvings.

450 **Standing 58 ft high it is the largest monolithic stone statue (built out of a single rock!) in the world.** Built around 983 CE, Gomateshwara, the son of the first Tirthankara or saviour, whom Jain devotees believe in, stands on a hill in the Jain temple complex at Shravanabelagola in Karnataka. Once in 12 years during '*mahamastak-abhisheka*' ceremonies, the enormous statue is bathed in milk, curd, ghee, saffron and gold coins, using high platforms and ladders.

451 **Artisans working on the minutely carved pillars, walls and ceilings of the five Dilwara Temples in Mount Abu, Rajasthan, were paid by the quantity of marble dust collected.** The temples are dedicated to five Tirthankaras. Built between the 11th and 13th centuries over 14 years, the complex's oldest temple is dedicated to Adinath, the first Tirthankara.

Dilwara Temples

452 **Some 1444 exquisitely carved amber and marble pillars hold up the Ranakpur Jain temples in Rajasthan.** They change colour from gold to blue, depending on the time of day. Dedicated to the first Tirthankara, Adinath, the

48,000 sq. ft building is also called a '*chaumukha*' temple, because it has a four-faced facade with four entrances.

453 **On Mount Shatrunjaya in Palitana in Gujarat, India, is a cluster of 863 exquisitely carved marble temples dedicated to the Tirthankaras.** Built over 900 years, from the 11th to the 20th centuries, the complex is a two-hour climb. The temple with a four-faced statue of Adinath, facing all four directions, takes 4,000 steps to get to. Interestingly, no one – not even the priests – can sleep over on the hill, as it is considered God's home.

Temples of Palitana

454 **An amazing cluster of mud and wood huts in the shape of a honeycomb form the Phuktal Monastery in Zanskar in Ladakh, Jammu and Kashmir, India.** Built at the mouth of a cave and reached by a suspension bridge over a river, the monastery houses 70 Buddhist monks. Founded by Gangsem Sherap Sampo sometime in the 12th century, it remained untouched by civilization till it was discovered in 1826. With writings carved on rocks and stupas along the way, it is reached, through Himalayan passes, by an eight-hour trek from the nearest town.

455 **The Taung Kalat monastery in Myanmar sits atop an extinct volcanic plug caused by the nearby volcano Mount Popa. Reached by 777 steps, it is home to 37 spirits called 'Nats' whose statues line the bottom of the steps.**

456 **Paintings, carvings and Buddhist sculptures are found among the 30 rock-cut Ajanta caves in Aurangabad in Maharashtra, India.** Carved into a 250 ft wall of rock, the caves consist of viharas or monasteries, stupa halls or chambers, and pictorial depictions of the lives and rebirths of the Buddha plus the Jataka tales and much more, all masterpieces of Buddhist religious art. Built in the 2nd century, the caves were discovered by chance in 1819 by British soldiers.

457 **More than 1,000 years old and still going strong is the Kye monastery in Spiti Valley in Himachal Pradesh, India.** In 2000, it celebrated the famous 'Kalchakra' celebration conducted once in a thousand years. Over 15,000 Buddhist monks, lamas and devotees from all over the world, including the Dalai Lama, attended it.

458 **The famous Taktsang (Tiger's Nest) Monastery in Bhutan sits on the edge of a 3,000 ft high cliff in Paro Valley.** Guru Rinpoche, who introduced Buddhism to Bhutan, flew on to a cliff, riding a tigress, to kill a demon and meditate in the cave, which is now part of this monastery. Built in 1692 and restored in 1998 it can be reached only by foot and has 13 tiger lairs or caves where Buddhist master Guru Padmasambhava is said to have meditated.

Tiger's Nest Monastery

20

TOWERS

Tall free-standing structures in which nobody lives, like minarets, observation towers and TV towers are defined as 'towers'. Most towers become tourist spots, mostly because of one or the other unusual architectural element.

459 **With 296 steps and a tilt, the famous Leaning Tower of Pisa is a bell tower in the cathedral premises in Pisa, Italy.** It took almost three centuries to build. It has seven bells in the bell chamber at the top, with one bell for each musical note. Due to a poorly laid and shallow foundation, the tower began to sink in 1173. Construction was stopped twice in between and the tower was completed only in 1372. The higher floors were built with one side taller than the other to compensate for the tilt and the tower is two steps short on one side! Now eight storeys high, it is a bit shorter than 183 ft on the higher and 93 ft on the lower side. Why hasn't it toppled over completely, though? During its restoration

Leaning Tower of Pisa (1890s)

between 1990 and 2001, the north-side foundations were dug out and the tilt was lessened by half a degree. In 2008, scientists said that the movement had finally stopped and the tower, now leaning at only 3.9 degrees, is expected to stay put for at least 200 years.

Belem Tower (1831)

460 **Belem Tower in Lisbon, Spain, was built in the early 16th century as part of the city's defence system. Several navigators set out from here to discover new trade routes.**

461 **A 220 ft high medieval cone-capped stone tower in Galata in Istanbul, Turkey, is a striking sight all along the river Bosphorus.** Originally known as the Tower of Christ, it was built in 1348 as part of the fortifications in Constantinople. It became famous when a man named Celebi attached wings to his arms and jumped off the tower! He is said to have flown a few miles on to the Bosphorus Sea and landed in the Dogancilar Square in Uskudar, with the help of the wind. Rope-climbing competitions are held regularly to the tower's top, which gives a magnificent view of Istanbul and the Bosphorus.

Qutub Minar (c. 1890)

462 In 1192, **Qutubuddin Aibak, the founder of the Delhi Sultanate, decided to build the tallest tower ever but completed only one storey.** The 237.8 ft high Qutub Minar in Mehrauli in Delhi, India, with 379

steps in a spiral staircase to the top, is the world's tallest brick minaret. In 1220, Aibak's successor and son-in-law, Shamsuddin Iltutmish, completed three more storeys. In 1369, a lightning strike destroyed the top storey, which Firoz Shah Tughlaq replaced, and added one more. Sher Shah Suri added an entrance to this five-storey tower. It is known for its rounded flutings, projecting balconies and calligraphy.

463 **A 213 ft high minaret, the Minaret of Jam, built entirely of baked bricks around 1190, is still standing.** Far away from any town, it is the oldest surviving tower in the world, near the rivers Jam and Hari in western Afghanistan. The minaret is famous for its intricate brick, stucco and glazed tile facade that has circular bands of ancient Islamic calligraphy, geometric patterns and Quranic verses. Though a UNESCO heritage site, it is on the verge of collapse due to decades of neglect and frequent floods.

464 French civil engineer **Gustave Eiffel designed a wrought-iron lattice tower 1063 ft tall and as high as an 81-storey building in Paris, France, in 1889.** Built for the Exposition Universelle to commemorate the centenary of the French Revolution, it became known as the Eiffel Tower. For the next 40 years, till the Chrysler Building was built in 1930 in the USA, this tower was the tallest structure in the world. As many as18,038 pieces of wrought iron with three and a half million rivets hold it together. The names of the 72 engineers who helped build it are engraved on it. Its iron structure weighs 7,300 tonnes and the total weight is 10,100 tonnes. It needs 50 to 60 tons of paint every seven years! It has 1,665 steps to the summit, but visitors have

to use elevators to its restaurants and the 906 ft high observation deck.

465 **Modern towers are either 'guyed' (with 'guy' wires tethered to the ground to stay up), such as transmission towers, or are 'free-standing' (without wires).** Free-standing towers are generally shorter than guyed towers. For guyed towers above 2,000 ft the anchors holding the guy wires are 0.8 km apart, so one needs a lot of land to build them.

466 **Svaneti in Georgia, eastern Europe, has famous towers built for defence, dating back to the 9th century CE. Each family here had its own tower! People climbed a rope stair, and pulled it up behind them, against enemies and heavy snowfall.**

467 **The KVLY-TV mast in Blanchard, North Dakota, USA, at 2,063 ft, is the tallest structure in the western hemisphere and the fourth-tallest structure in the world.** This guyed tower rises up like a needle. It's so narrow that it's just a vertical line on the horizon until you get close. Built in 1963, it was the tallest structure in the world for many years.

468 **The CN Tower is Canada's most recognizable symbol.** This communications – radio and TV – tower took 40 months to build and was completed in 1976. Built by the railway company Canadian National, it is1815.4 ft tall and was the tallest structure in the world for over 30 years till the Burj Khalifa was built in Dubai! In 1995, it was declared one of the modern Seven Wonders of the World by the American Society of Civil Engineers. It has 1,776 steps and 144 flights to the top. A restaurant here at 1,151 ft, called 360 Degrees, has the highest wine cellar in the world! The Edge Walk here is the world's highest hands-free walk on a

5 ft wide ledge encircling the top of the tower at 1168 ft, about 116 storeys above the ground.

Space Needle observation tower

469 **Shaped like a spaceship, the Space Needle observation tower in Seattle, USA, is a landmark with an amazing structure.** It is 605 ft high, 138 ft wide, and weighs 8,660 tonnes. It is built to withstand winds of up to 320 kmph and earthquakes of up to 9.0 magnitude. It also has an observation deck at 520 ft and a rotating Sky City restaurant at 500 ft height. A trip to the top takes 41 seconds. It also has the world's first and only revolving glass floor, known as 'The Loupe'.

470 **The Ostankino Tower in Moscow, Russia, is currently the tallest free-standing structure in Europe and the seventh tallest in the world.** The 1,772 ft high tower opened in 1967 as a TV and radio tower. When built, it was the first free-standing structure to go over 1,600 ft in height. The Ostankino TV & BC Tower transmits the signals of 11 TV stations, 12 radio stations and 17 satellite TV programmes. It is the largest multi-function communications structure in the world.

471 **The sandstone Spiral Minaret or Malwiya Minaret, part of the Great Mosque of Samarra in Iraq, has a unique ascending spiral conical design. Built during 848–52 CE, it was originally connected to the mosque by a bridge. The tower is 162 ft high. In 2005, militants blew up its top section.**

472 **The 709 ft Zizkov TV tower on a hill in Mahler Gardens in Prague, Hungary, was once voted the second ugliest**

473 **Built in 1994, the Oriental Pearl TV Tower in Shanghai, China, stands 1,535 ft tall and was once the tallest tower in Shanghai.** One of its three observation decks, at 850 ft, has a glass-bottomed floor that gives you the feeling of floating directly above the river Huangpo below. It is made up of 11 differently sized spheres linked by three 22.9 ft columns. The highest sphere is 46 ft in diameter. The three large spheres form the space module, with the large lower one boasting of a futuristic science-fantasy space city. The five smaller ones are a hotel with 25 elegant rooms and lounges. The remaining three spheres are decorative ones. The entire structure rests on rich green grass lawns and looks like precious gems on a green salver. It is a TV and radio tower with more than nine TV channels and ten FM radio channels. The Municipal History Museum is located in the tower's pedestal.

building in the world in an online poll conducted by VirtualTourist.com. (The ugliest one was Morris A. Mechanic Theatre in Baltimore, USA, which has since been demolished.) At 709 ft, the Zizkov was completed in 1992. It has startling bronze statues of babies crawling up and down it, made by artist David Cerny. It is an unconventional tower based on a triangle whose corners go up in steel columns filled with concrete. They support nine 'pods' and three decks for transmitting equipment.

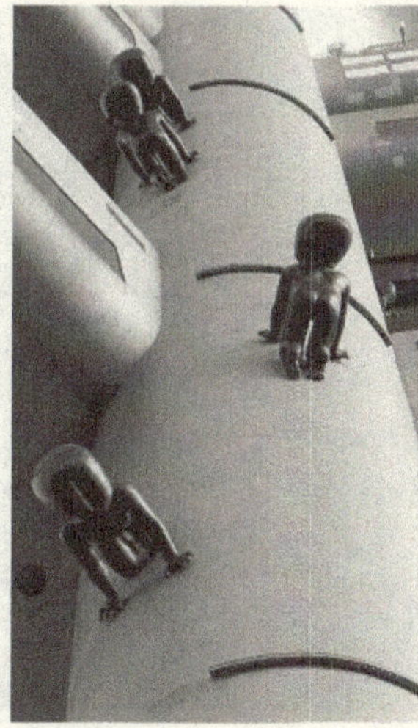

474 **With high-powered binoculars and interactive touch-screens, the Sydney Tower Eye is the tallest building in Sydney, Australia.** While its observation tower stands at 1,014 ft, its 'Skywalk', with its open-air, glass-floor viewing platform is 879 ft above the city streets. The golden turret near the top can accommodate 960 people. Built in 2005, its three high-speed double-deck lifts take you to the observation floor. The Sydney Tower Stair Challenge is held here every year. Runners have to sprint up 1,504 stairs to the observation deck to raise money for the Cancer Council, and the two winners become eligible to compete in the Empire State Building run-up in the USA.

475 **Built in 1958, the Tokyo Tower is one of the best-known towers in the world.** It is 1,092 feet tall and made of prefabricated steel, which makes it relatively light at only 4,000 tonnes. All of Tokyo's TV broadcasts and four FM radio stations are transmitted throughout the city from this 'lattice'-

Tokyo Tower

design tower, based on the Eiffel Tower. The 164 floodlights installed all over the tower give it an ethereal look at night.

476 **Berlin's most recognizable landmark, the Fernsehturm, was modelled on the Sputnik satellite (launched in 1957 by Soviet Russia).** This 1,207 ft high tower was nicknamed the 'Pope's revenge' as the shape of a cross appears on the building when the sun shines on the round dome of this TV tower. Built in 1969, it has 986 steps and a rotating restaurant that takes 30 minutes to give a 360-degree view of Germany's capital city. To avoid emergencies, the kitchen is at the base of the Tower and every dish travels up hundreds of feet in a special elevator. Deutsche Telekom broadcasts more than 60 TV and radio programmes via its antenna.

477 **The New Tokyo Sky Tree in Tokyo, Japan, is made entirely of steel. Opened in 2010, this broadcasting and observation tower in Sumida is 2,080 ft high. It is the tallest tower in the world after the Burj Khalifa.**

478 **The Petronas Twin Towers in Kuala Lumpur, Malaysia, are the tallest twin towers in the world.** The 1,483 ft and 88-storey high towers feature geometric patterns inspired by Islamic architecture in a pattern repeated all over them. Designed by Cesar Pelli, the towers are occupied by offices. A skybridge, very popular with tourists, connects the towers.

21

UNUSUAL BUILDINGS

Many people have turned their flights of fancy into reality by constructing buildings that combine imagination and determination! And these weird and wonderful structures can be found all around the world...

479 **Drop in at Toon Town in either of the two Disneys– Wonderland in California or Disney World in Orlando – to meet Minnie Mouse, the animated celebrity.** Minnie Mouse House, all in pink and lilac, has a heart-shaped gate too in a pink picket fence. Inside, it is even more fun with a cake actually baking and a microwave that can make stuff go pop.

480 **Kaufman and Broad homebuilders built a replica of the 'Simpsons House' (742 Evergreen Terrace) in 1997 in Henderson, Nevada and offered it up as a prize in a contest.** They watched 100 episodes of the animated series and took 49 days to perfect the house. More than 30,000 people visited it, including 'The Simpsons' creator Matt Groening, and 15 million people entered the contest. The 2200 sq. ft house had, among 1,500 other Simpsons' related items, Homer's large TV-room sofa, the checkered linoleum floor in the kitchen, the tree house, a swing set and the back yard barbecue. It cost USD 120,000 to build.

However, the winner, Barbara Howard, took it stripped off of all the Simpson paraphernalia.

481 **In Manchester, UK, the Royal Exchange Theatre resembles a lunar landing module and is suspended from four piers that support the huge dome. It looks so authentic that you could be fooled into believing it really is one.**

482 **A house in Hillsborough, California, is modelled on the Flintstone family home in the cartoon series.** Built with wire mesh frames and air-filled balloons, Flintstone House is a 2,700 sq. ft house of orange-painted domes with floors of rocks instead of tiles. Architect William Nicholson visualized the Flintstones living in a home that had three bedrooms, a spiral staircase and, yes, a two-car garage.

483 **Like standing on your head? Then you might just get to do that in this Upside Down House in Terfens in Tyrol, Austria.** Two Polish architects spent eight months building a house 'upside down', where everything from the cutlery and the furniture is the other way round to normal. Even the car is stuck upside down!

The Upside-Down House

484 **Batman's Garage in Toorak in Melbourne, Australia comes complete with jazzy vehicles.** A luxury home called 'The Wayne Manor' has a secret entrance under a tennis court and a sloped driveway that descends into

what could be a modern-day Batcave, based on the movie, *The Dark Knight*. It even has a hydraulically powered lift that reveals a ramp underneath the tennis court which is under the mansion. A staircase to the garage sits under the living-room floor.

485 **A replica of the little hut that book character Heidi the Swiss girl lived in with her grandfather is still around in Switzerland.** It is located in the village of Ober Rofels, now called Heidi Village, which is complete with wandering goats. Lived in until 1997, it is a rural 300-year-old stone and wood hut with a cellar, a front room, Grandfather's room, Heidi's room, and an attic. It has been restored and furnished so that it appears as it did in the book in 1880, the time during which Johanna Spyri's Heidi story takes place.

486 **Israel has some unusual beehive houses!** Architect Zvi Hecker designed a public housing project, called the Honey Bee Hive House, in Jerusalem. With an upside-down geometric design, it had some 720 prefabricated units all stuck into each other. This inspired British architect Barry Jackson to create another bee-hived model – the HIVEHAUS design – where an entire home can be built by connecting each individual honeycomb room to the other until the house is just as big as you want it.

487 **The National Fisheries Development Board in India imaginatively designed themselves a fish-shaped building in Hyderabad.** In 2012, they came up with the four-storey office building called Matsya Bhavan, on five acres of land. They were apparently inspired by the

famous architect Frank Gehry's huge sculpture 'Fish' in Barcelona, Spain.

488 **The amazing Heliodome, a bio-climatic solar house in Cosswiller in eastern France, is shaped like a cut diamond.** Designed as a three-dimensional sundial, it keeps the temperature cool during summer and warm in winter. Imagine, no electricity bills!

489 **There is a Skateboard House, the vision of Pierre Andre Senizergues (PAS), a former skateboarding world champion, in Malibu, California!** In this house, one can skateboard on any area and surface, indoors and outdoors. The floor, wall and ceiling merge in an uninterrupted surface, forming a tube. Even the furniture is skate-able.

490 **It doesn't qualify as a building nor is it an unusual piece of architecture but in Lima, Peru, is a 17th century bridge which is still standing.** Called the Bridge of Eggs it was made of mortar that was mixed not with water but with the whites of 10,000 seabird eggs, which is what qualifies it to be called remarkable.

491 **In New Zealand's small town of Tirau, guarding the highway is man's best friend in the form of a building made of corrugated iron.** A big sheep and a big ram keep the dog company. The Big Dog building houses an information centre while the Big Sheep has wool and craft shops in its stomach. Made of corrugated iron, it was designed by Steven Clothier in 1990. The town also has a cow with a shopping cart, a shepherd outside a church and a praying mantis made of corrugated iron.

Big Dog and Big Sheep

492 **Designed by Hefei University of Technology, The Piano House in Anhui, China, is an unusually beautiful building considering it has a large violin resting against an equally large piano.** The transparent violin allows you a grand view of the escalators and the staircase within. The piano, on the other hand, is a government showroom. It is now more popular as a tourist attraction.

493 **As the light hits it, the Nautilus Giant Seashell House in Mexico City, Mexico, glows bright. Designed and built by Javier Senosiain in 2006, the front of the modern house is clad with coloured mosaics.**

494 **Designed by architect Antoni Gaudi, the fairy-tale Mind House in Barcelona, Spain, is part of the famous Park Guell.** Standing on 37 acres, two gingerbread houses – one with a toadstool on top and the other with a toadstool cum cross-shaped window on the front wall – guard the entrance. With a white and grey checked roof it has three floors and an attic. A wide staircase outside the gates takes you to the terrace-cum-roof embedded in the hill. There is a huge mosaic lizard as well. It is a popular museum.

495 **Tucked away in Portugal's Fafe hills is the Casa do Penedo, meaning House of the Rock.** Built in 1972, this **Stone House** is a prehistoric-looking structure made up of four large boulders going one into each other to form the foundation, walls and ceiling of the house. Made entirely of stone except for the windows and door frames, it has a 350 kg couch built from a large eucalyptus tree. Inspired by the Flintstone house, it was initially a holiday home but is now a museum. But it has no electricity.

496 **Encouraged by popular Polish fairy-tale illustrations, the Crooked House or Krzywy Domek in Sopot, Poland, is a thoroughly amusing building.** All higgledy-piggledy, it is a 4,000 sq. ft building that is part of a shopping complex. Built in 2004, it houses many popular shops, restaurants and even a radio station.

497 **In the village of Miziara in Lebanon is a house that resembles an Airbus 380.** It has two floors with some 40 portholes on each side, and a short and round nose cone. Everything from an impressive living room, to bedrooms, to a spiral staircase, the **Airplane House** has it all. It belongs to a Lebanese family that lives in Australia.

498 **Le Palais Ideal in the small town of Hauterives near Lyon in France is the unique dream of Ferdinand Cheval (1836–1924), a rural postman.** On one his rounds, he tripped over a stone and was so charmed by its unusual shape that he decided to build a palace so imaginative that tourists now flock to it. Though he was completely inexperienced

in this field, he built it all by himself, bearing the taunts of people in the early days of his project. The palace includes many architectural styles, such as the Chinese, Algerian and Northern European, to create a fantastical castle of grottoes, around 85 ft long and 32.5 ft high. There is even a 'Temple Hindou' (Hindu Temple')! It took Cheval 33 years to make this with stones he found and bound with lime, mortar and cement to construct a palace inhabited by sculpted animals, fairies, gods and mythological figures from all over the world.

Le Palais Ideal

499 **Built in 1958 for the Brussels World Fair, the 334.6 ft high Atomium in Belgium houses restaurants, offices and halls. It has nine (59 ft diameter) stainless-steel-clad spheres connected together by (9.8 ft diameter) tubes to mimic the basic cell of an iron crystal, and looks like a futuristic spaceship.**

500 **The Cybertecture Egg is an oval 13-storey building in Mumbai, India, which has restrooms that automatically monitor and measure your weight and blood pressure, and electronically transmit it to doctors. Opened in 2010, and designed by James Law, it is a smart building!**

501 **The Basket Building in Ohio, USA, is a seven-storey tall, 180,000 sq. ft structure in the shape of an actual big basket. Designed by the basket-making Longaberger**

The Basket Building

Company as their office, the basket handle in itself weighs almost 150 tonnes. Built in 1997 on 22 acres of land, it can be heated during winter to prevent damage from ice.